SYDNEY by Ferry & Foot

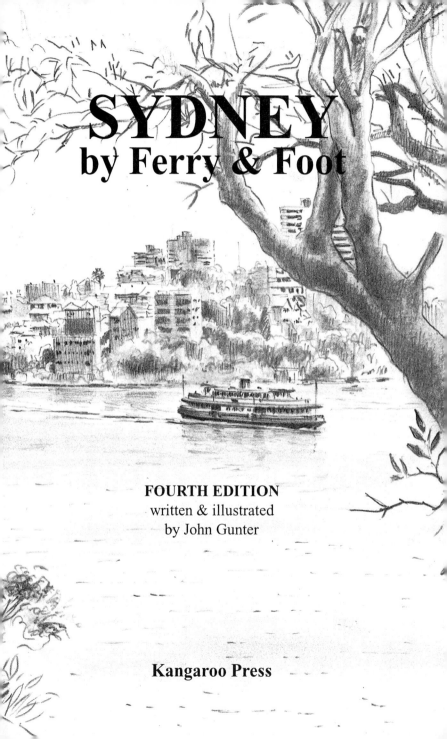

SYDNEY
by Ferry & Foot

FOURTH EDITION
written & illustrated
by John Gunter

Kangaroo Press

Fourth edition published 1995
First published in 1983 by Kangaroo Press Pty Ltd
3 Whitehall Road Kenthurst NSW 2156 Australia
P.O. Box 6125 Dural Delivery Centre NSW 2158
Printed by Star Printery, Erskineville

ISBN 0 86417 621 X

Cover design by Darian Causby

Contents

Acknowledgments

This is a book I've wanted to write for a long time. Mostly because I've done nearly all these trips before, and loved them. For some I set out from home and others from workplaces. Luckily, from the earliest school holiday times, I'd always find someone to wander along the footpaths and bush tracks with me.

So thanks David, Cabby, Terry, Ted, Sue, Gaz and Jane for sharing those good days, and special thanks to the late Vetta Mesmer, my Dad, for all our walks and all the talks!

Also of course lots of people helped with the hard part, the gathering of information and material for the book. So to Van and Mary McCune, Cabby Gunter, Gary and Mitch, Boo Johnson, Greg Travers, John Darroch, Bill Allen, John Mathieson and Mr Wilson of the Royal Botanic Gardens, go my special thanks. I'm also most grateful to the staff of the Manly, Hunters Hill, Mosman and North Sydney Libraries and Councils and to the staff of Balmain Library. I appreciate the help too from the Australian Gas Light Company, the Australian Museum, the Senior Ranger of the Sydney Harbour National Park, and Susan Thompson of the State Transit Authority.

Very special thanks to the late Elsie Coleman for typing the manuscript.

Introduction

With some Helpful Hints on the Walks

Visitors to Sydney today mostly arrive by air. What a shame. I think the only way to understand this city—her beauty, character, soul if you like—is to approach by sea.

Fortunately, though, we can recreate a good part of that understanding by ferry—whether by rolling across the Heads to Manly, or gliding into the quiet bays and coves of this truly magnificent Sydney Harbour.

So to set the mood for each of these explorations we will arrive by water—on a ferry boat.

Having done that, the major part of each trip is the walk.

These vary from less than an hour to nearly all day, from smooth footpaths to exploring the actual waterfront, and in some places jumping from rock to rock.

The best type of clothing and footwear will be mentioned if it differs from normal casual wear.

Weekday mornings are usually the best time to walk, as most places will be almost deserted and afternoons can be too shady and windy. However, weekends are fine for those who can't manage otherwise. Indeed, Saturday and Sunday on Sydney Harbour with thousands of sailing craft competing for a few metres of water and a few centimetres of column space in the sports results, is really something.

A small backpack or shoulder bag is good for the longer walks, as kiosks and shops are often closed and a snack or picnic lunch, with perhaps a bottle of wine or soft drink, could make the day complete.

Almost all the bush we pass through is part of the Sydney Harbour National Park, so no dogs are allowed, and as rangers patrol it is advisable to leave your animals at home. Bring your own gas-type fire if you want to cook lunch; otherwise no fires or camping are permitted.

This then is a book to help you discover the real Sydney—city, harbour, suburbs and bush. From concrete to sand, from exhaust fumes to ozone. It's for residents and visitors alike, who perhaps have looked, but haven't seen.

It's the mid 1930s and here are two of Sydney's biggest ferries: *Kuttabul* and *Koompartoo*. The latter has had her wheelhouses raised for use as a 'showboat'.

The Ferry Boats of Sydney
A Brief History

Sails and oars propelled Sydney's first ferry, *The Rose Hill Packet,* launched in 1789. She ran with passengers and goods up the river to Parramatta, the trip sometimes taking a week!

Several decades later Governor Macquarie appointed a Jamaican, Billy Blue (later known as the Old Commodore), to provide Sydney town with a cross-harbour ferry service. It ran from Dawes Point near where the southern Bridge pylons are today, to Blues Point, named for Billy himself. It was no more than a large rowing boat, but this was 1830.

Steam arrived shortly after and various vessels and companies ran excursions and eventually regular trips.

The real beginning, however, was in 1861 when the North Shore Ferry Company was formed. By 1899 it had become Sydney Ferries Limited and such was the explosion of population and travel that only ten years later in 1909 the company's 51 ferries carried over 40 million passengers!

By the 1920s, Sydney Ferries Limited had taken over all its main competitors (except the strong Manly and Port Jackson Steamship Company) and the wake of their huge fleet could be seen in all parts of the harbour.

Henry Gilbert Smith subdivided his Manly land and put it up for sale back in 1853, chartering a ferry, *The Brothers,* to bring the prospective customers. Soon the area became justifiably popular and many boats were pressed into service to transport day trippers to sun and sand.

Since the 1850s a regular weekday service has operated, and during the early 1890s rival companies fought for a slice of the trade, until nobody was making any money. They finally amalgamated in 1896.

The forerunner of the modern Manly ferry was the locally designed and built 1228 passenger *Kuring-gai* of 1901. Although not as plush as the imported paddler *Brighton,* she was more economical and had the benefit of electric light which 'will serve at all times as well as the beautiful but inconsistent moon'!

Six more of similar design were built at Morts Dock. They were the approximately 1500 passenger *Binngarra* (1905), *Burra-Bra* (1908), *Bellubera* (1910), *Balgowlah* (1912), *Barrenjoey* (1913—later *North Head)*, and *Baragoola* (1922). The Port Jackson and Manly Steamship Company of those times really did take people 'seven miles from Sydney and a thousand miles from care' as stated in their motto.

From 1900 until 1926 Sydney Ferries Limited built seven vehicular ferries or punts to cater for the ever increasing lines of waiting traffic. Trains and trams brought hoards of people to Milsons Point at North Sydney, where they poured into the biggest ferries ever to run in the harbour service. Boats such as 1250 passenger *Kai Kai* (1907), 1360 passenger *Kuramia* (1914) and the delightfully named 2500 passenger *Koompartoo* and sister *Kuttabul* (both of 1922). Within a few years they would be steaming across the lengthening shadow of the Sydney Harbour Bridge.

After the opening of the great span, Sydney Ferries struggled on by selling off some of the fleet and fitting economical diesel engines to others. The Manly company, not so affected, brought three new steamers into service between 1928 and 1930. They were the much loved 1587 passenger sisters *Curl Curl* and *Dee Why* and the magnificent 1781 passenger *South Steyne.*

During the Second World War the Australian and United States forces bought up many of the redundant ferries for use as accommodation, boom defence and store ships.

Circular Quay when funnels were tall

The last of the coal-fired ferries, *Kubu*. She was scrapped in 1959

Before padding or plastic, seats were like these on *Kanangra* of 1912

The curved centre windows, seen on the early screw-driven boats, were no doubt a design replacement for the redundant paddle boxes

HMAS *Kuttabul* was one such vessel, moored alongside Garden Island. On the night of 31 May 1942 Japanese midget submarines attacked Sydney Harbour and in the ensuing battle *Kuttabul* was blown up and sunk by a torpedo. Nineteen sailors died and ten more were injured.

After the war, business continued its decline for the ferry and tram services. Since just after the turn of the century trams had wound their way down most of the harbourside hills to meet the ferries. Now one of the world's largest tramway systems was in its last years of existence.

Sydney Ferries was taken over by the State government in 1951, who converted the few remaining steamers to oil engines. The last coal-fired steamer was *Kubu,* scrapped in November 1959.

In the same year tram services were being wound down as private transport and narrow streets became too hard to compete against. The last tram ran in February 1961.

In 1974 the Manly company sold its remaining two ferries and four hydrofoils to the State government, after the flagship *South Steyne* had been damaged by fire. She was sold 'as is' to private buyers. She has since been extensively rebuilt, but for Sydney an era had come to an end.

However, since 1976 governments have again been spending money on harbour transport, with new ferries and catamarans being built. The private sector too has drastically increased its fleet of cruise boats. So the scene is set for the 1990s to be the decade of belated rediscovery of one of the most beautiful waterways in the world. A new era has begun.

After almost 30 years' service, the hydrofoils were replaced by —

— The smooth riding (but wave making) jet cats

A Guide to Sydney Harbour

From Circular Quay to Manly and back

To help identify the various important parts of the Harbour we'll take a trip to Manly from Circular Quay. On the way out stand on the right hand, or starboard side, then change sides for the return trip to Sydney. This will save you moving from side to side as we progress.

This description will also suffice for the inner Harbour trips east of the Harbour Bridge.

Leaving Circular Quay, or Semi Circular Quay as it was known in 1844 when the stone surrounds were built, we head out into Sydney Cove proper and pass the Opera House on Bennelong Point (designed by Joern Utzon and opened by Her Majesty Queen Elizabeth II in 1973).

A winged dream come true

The big bay with the stone wall all around it, at the foot of the Royal Botanic Gardens, is Farm Cove, where the first crops for the original colony of Sydney Town were grown. On the western side of the bay, behind the Opera House and visible above the trees, are the castellated walls of Government House. This is the residence of the State Governor. *(See Trip 8.)*

On the other side of the bay is Mrs Macquarie's Point, where in 1816 Governor Macquarie had a roadway and a seat built in the sandstone rock. This was to enable his good wife 'the better to enjoy the view'.

We'll break our starboard side rule here and cross over to the other side for a look at Fort Denison or 'Pinchgut'. Some say the name derives from a nautical term for the narrowing of a body of water at a certain place, perhaps like this part of Sydney Harbour. Another explanation could be that on 8 February 1788 at the first criminal court hearing, a convict was sentenced to the then rocky pinnacle for having stolen biscuits. He was to stay there on bread and water for a week. Others followed, also on meagre rations which were literally gut-pinchers!

The stone martello tower was built in 1856, when fear of a Russian invasion caused its addition to the then half-finished fort.

Visits can be arranged by telephone on 206 1130.

'Pinchgut' or Fort Denison

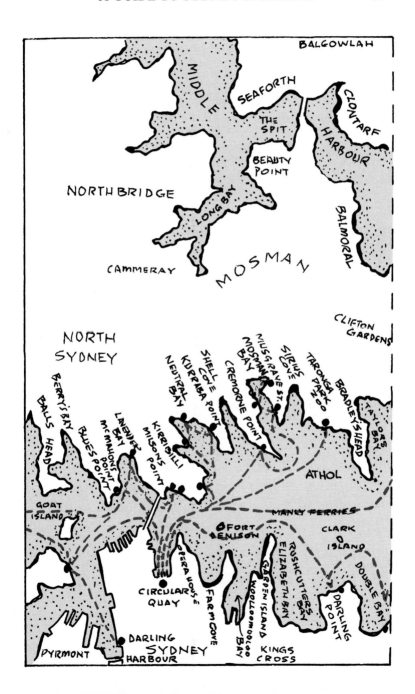

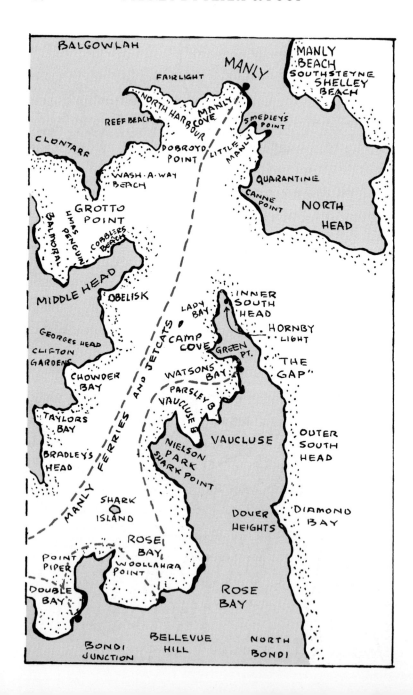

Cross back now to see Woolloomooloo (which must have the most beautiful sounding name in Sydney) on the eastern side of which is the Garden Island Naval Depot. This is dominated by a large hammerhead crane, capable of a 250-tonne lift, and nearby is a dry dock built to take ships as large as the once proud 83 000 tonne *Queen Elizabeth.* The construction of the dock joined the island to the mainland. Above and behind are the flats and hotels of Potts Point. The Garden part of the name comes from the first settlers, who cultivated the island for their home grown vegetables.

The next bay is Elizabeth and the maze of yacht masts to its left is actually in Rushcutters Bay. This is the home of the Cruising Yacht Club of Australia, which organises the Sydney to Hobart Race each year, and where 'rushcutters' cut the reeds for the roofs of early Sydney houses.

Behind Clark Island is Darling Point, then Double Bay and Point Piper, with a prominent block of flats and several tall units. Next is Woollahra Point, and stretching around to the left is the large curve of Sydney's biggest bay, Rose Bay. From here flying boats once droned up the harbour heading for many foreign shores, long before land planes finally took over the role of international passenger carriers.

Shark Island sits fairly unobtrusively out in the Harbour waiting for picnickers, while behind and to the north, bush leads down past Shark Point to Neilson Park, with its beach and shark-proof net. On the sky-line above is a water tower.

Around the rocks of Vaucluse Point are Vaucluse and Parsley Bays, with the white South Head Macquarie Lighthouse above, and a little white bridge below in Parsley Bay. *(See Trip 13.)*

The big bay following is Watson's Bay, the traditional home of the port's pilot boats and seafood restaurants. The bay is in fact named for the first Sydney pilot, Robert Watson. The grass-covered headland is Green Point, from which, during the Second World War, a net or boom was stretched to Georges Head opposite, to stop enemy shipping and submarines.

The reef that separates the eastern and western shipping lanes or channels is known as Sow and Pigs, and 'covers' at half tide. This shipping hazard is marked by three black and yellow buoys with two inverted triangles at the top. The reef is often used as a 'mark' in sailing races, as is the white light beacon off Watson's Bay which is known as the 'Wedding Cake'.

Below all the buildings at Inner South Head is Camp Cove and the last beach on the eastern shore is Lady Bay (sometimes called Lady Jane Bay), home to nude swimmers south of the Bridge.

Now as we start to cross the Heads (the distance between them is 1500 metres) we can see the red and white striped unmanned Hornby Light. It was built in 1858 to indicate the entrance to Sydney Harbour, after the wreck of the *Dunbar* there a year before. She had smashed into the cliffs near 'The Gap' during a south-easterly gale. Of the 122 people on board, 121 died in the tragedy.

On the north side of the Heads on the Harbour side is Canne Point (Aboriginal name Canna) which is part of the entrance to North Harbour. Above are scattered the remaining buildings of the old Quarantine Station (opened in 1837). Unused now owing to the effectiveness of modern drugs, it was last used to house refugees from Darwin's Cyclone 'Tracy' in 1974. (Now part of National Parks.)

Below is Quarantine Beach, then Store Beach, and in the corner Spring Cove. It is believed that this is where Governor Phillip was speared by a frightened Aborigine in 1790.

Next is Little Manly Point and Cove *(see Trip 7)* and at the entrance to Manly Cove is Manly Point, with the twin round home units nearby on Smedleys Point. Then we dock at Manly Wharf, almost in the centre of Manly Cove.

For the return journey, change sides and face west and as the ferry moves out we can see the suburbs of Fairlight, Balgowlah, and behind the yachts, Forty Baskets Beach (see Trips 5 and 6). The strip of sand amid rocks and bush is the nudists' own Reef Beach. Dobroyd Head is next, up high, and below is Dobroyd Point, all part of Sydney Harbour National Park. Just to the south are three yellow and black bombora buoys which warn of a submerged reef, where waves can quickly rise and break. Two Harbour surveyors were drowned here in 1874.

The bushy headland with a little lighthouse at its end and Wash-a-way beach at its beginning, is Grotto Point. Behind are houses, home units and flats, heading down the Mosman slopes to Balmoral Beach *(see Trip 4)* and around to the Naval Depot, HMAS *Penguin* and Cobblers Beach.

Around the eroded arm of Middle Head with its old gun emplacements and tall radio masts is Obelisk Bay, with two white obelisks visible. One is low by the water and the other half way up the hill behind, in the bush. These were used by shipping as 'leads' into the Harbour. When they were lined up with each other it was safe to proceed and find the correct channel. Below is Obelisk Beach.

On the northern side of the next headland, Georges Head, notice the gun holes cut into the rocks for the protection of the port during wartime. The buildings visible around the corner are army buildings which extend to Clifton Gardens, where there's a large swimming pool and park in Chowder Bay *(see Trip 3).*

Just around Chowder Head, tucked in among the trees is Mosman's biggest house, 'The Manor', its many roof peaks towering above sheltered Taylor Bay. Then follow the long decline of the ridge with its dead trees, to Bradley's Head. At the Point is the mast or fighting top of the light cruiser *Sydney,* which sank the German cruiser *Emden* in 1914.

Looking west from Bradley's Head

Around the corner is Athol Bay or Bight. Behind, high up, is the Zoo, its wharf below, then Whiting Beach, Sirius Cove and Cremorne Point.

In the area between Cremorne Point and Bradleys Head once floated the biggest passenger ships ever built. It was during war time, so huge vessels such as *Queen Elizabeth* and *Queen Mary* lay waiting at anchor, ready to speed thousands of troops to countries involved in the hostilities. In the suburbs around the harbour warships too waited, tied to wooden 'dolphins', quickly erected in bays and coves to take the extra ships.

After Cremorne Point is Shell Cove, then Kurraba Point with a little green park where the Manly Ferry depot once was. The bay to the west is Neutral Bay, for here, early in Sydney's history, foreign ships could lie unmolested (also away from the convicts, so preventing any attempt at their escape to sea).

Hidden away on the western side of Neutral Bay is Careening Cove, and on Kirribilli Headland at the point, is Admiralty House (1846) so named because from 1885 until 1913 it was home to British admirals who were in command of the Australian fleet. Its present function is that of the Sydney residence of the Australian Governor General. Behind to the north is pretty Kirribilli House (1855), used by the Federal Government for VIPs, including the Prime Minister, when in Sydney.

Kirribilli, with Admiralty House and Kirribilli House

Now we sweep around into Sydney Cove again in front of the splendid steel spars and arch of the Harbour Bridge *(see Trip 9)*, built in 1932, past wharves and the Overseas Passenger Terminal of 1961, where the world's longest passenger liner, *France,* docked in 1974, while underwater to our left is the Sydney Harbour Tunnel.

Finally, we drift into the wharf at the Quay having finished our journey over to Manly, which was always known to be 'seven miles from Sydney and a thousand mile from care'.

Along the Shores of Mosman Bay

*From naughty old Cremorne Point to where
whales once were*

Type of Terrain

Mostly level to undulating with only a few stairs. Sealed for the whole
distance. Suitable for wheelchairs and strollers, although assistance
would be necessary at the various stairs. There are three lots of three
and one of twelve.

Degree of difficulty 2/10

Summary

An easy, pleasant walk on pavement with both sweeping and intimate
views, having water and bush on one side and civilisation on the other.

Old Cremorne with old Karingal

Time

Allow approximately one slow hour.

Clothes

No special needs, but remember that the Sydney sun can burn quickly, so a hat and sunscreen are always wise.

Ferry Departure Details

Ferries don't necessarily leave from the same jetties on weekends as they do on weekdays, or run to the same timetables, so it is always best to check with the Ferry Information Kiosk (opposite No. 4 Jetty) or ring the number listed in the current telephone book if you are in any doubt as to departure times, jetties or destinations.

Note: Cremorne–Mosman ferries run approximately every half hour on weekdays and Saturdays, and hourly on Sundays.

The Walk

The walk follows the shore line of Cremorne Point and Mosman Bay, past mostly native bush on the harbour and bay side, with houses, flats and colourful gardens on the other. Several short tracks lead down to the rocks for secluded picnics, fishing, and at other than dead low tide, a quick swim. Best walked in the morning or early afternoon. There are swings and slippery dips for children also public lavatories, telephones, drinking bubblers and a shop. So let's go and explore.

After leaving the Cremorne Wharf, which has been here since the tram services opened in 1911, go across the road and climb the stairs opposite, except for our wheelchair-bound friends who will follow the main footpath left from the wharf a few hundred metres until a sign with Cremorne Reserve is reached. Cross over the road here to reach the driveway opposite, which will become the path that we would have joined had we climbed the stairs.

The Aboriginal name for this point is Goram-Bulla-Gong. In 1823 Governor Sir Thomas Brisbane granted the land to James Robertson for his services as scientific instrument repairer, and in 1853 it passed to the late James Milson. Three years later 22 acres (9 hectares) were

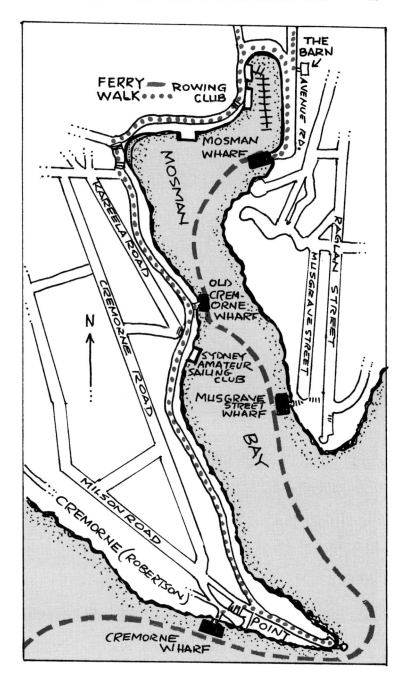

THE BARN

FERRY WALK — ROWING CLUB

AVENUE RD.

MOSMAN WHARF

MOSMAN

KAREELA ROAD

CREMORNE ROAD

RAGLAN STREET

MUSGRAVE STREET

N

OLD CREMORNE WHARF

SYDNEY AMATEUR SAILING CLUB

MUSGRAVE STREET WHARF

BAY

MILSON ROAD

CREMORNE (ROBERTSON)

POINT

CREMORNE WHARF

The ferry *Royale* passing the old lighthouse on Cremorne Point

The pathway near where Cremorne Gardens used to be

Angophora enjoying the sun in one of many cultivated gardens

leased to Messrs Clarke and Woolcott who turned the area into pleasure grounds and named it after the then famous Cremorne Gardens in England.

One could partake of dancing, shooting, archery and watch fireworks till the early hours. However, all was not as advertised, and the 'rougher element' of the day gave the area a bad name by their revelry 'which was not always the most decorous', so the area became run down and finally overgrown.

By 1881 the land was up for sale, and although coal was discovered two years later, mining was not undertaken on a commercial scale. This is fortunate for us today as one can enjoy the reasonably unspoiled headland that should be Robertson Point, but is better known as Cremorne Point. And that's where we'll go now.

Follow the path along past the public toilets and swings until the end of the point is reached and you are standing above a charming little lighthouse (erected about 1904) and no doubt several fishermen after bream or blackfish on the rocks below.

From here there are sweeping views of the city to the south west, Fort Denison or Pinchgut to the south, then the Eastern Suburbs, Rose Bay, Bradleys Head with its mast of the light cruiser HMAS *Sydney,* and Athol Bight where the famous *Queens* once anchored. To the North are the grounds and buildings of Taronga Zoological Park with its ferry wharf below. Next around is the usually flotsam covered Whiting Beach, and then the eroded headland of pretty Little Sirius Cove. The point with the rather large home units is Curraghbeena, and still further left is beautiful tranquil Mosman Bay. We'll explore the western shore which once sheltered Captain Arthur Phillip's flagship Sirius.

Mosman Bay (pronounced Moss-man and often misspelled this way) was selected in June 1789 as the place in which to careen HMS *Sirius,* and apart from any geographic reason it was favoured for the sailors because here they were 'less likely to meet with temptation to idleness and bad company'.

Now before we leave the point look around about and find a coral tree, many stands of which will be seen along the way. They have large green leaves in summer, but carry only masses of red flowers in winter, and often seen among the spiky boughs are rainbow lorikeets and large

Around the shores of Mosman Bay

sulphur crested cockatoos hopping and chattering about, gathering honey.

Retrace our steps now almost to where the steps from the wharf join the upper path near a bubbler (drinking fountain) and take the path to the extreme right passing houses and flats to the left, noticing on the right a good collection of Port Jackson fig trees near a short paved track which leads down to a workman's stone shed. Carrying on down the main path you'll see in a garden a typical *Angophora costata* that looks like a gum tree but isn't.

Shortly after on the bay side near another bubbler is a colourful garden. Further on, just past a pretty little gazebo, follow a path to Old Cremorne Wharf, leaving Sydney Amateur Sailing clubhouse and boat slips on the right, by going up three steps and following the fence to the wharf. From there, take the lower path which rises up to some steps.

Soon the end of the bay becomes visible, with the Mosman Amateur Sailing clubhouse and Mosman Rowing Club on the northern shore. Also visible is the yacht marina and Mosman Wharf. (Rosman's ferries moved from here in 1987.)

Keeping to the right the path splits three ways at a dense grove of trees. For easy walking, fewer steps and a better look at this pretty little valley, take the centre path and turn right down four steps and over a little bridge, staying to the right. A short distance down the track, about when Cremorne Point becomes clearly visible, look to the right towards Old Cremorne Wharf. On the water's edge, approximately in line with a pine tree, a large rock with a rusty ringbolt can (with some difficulty) be seen. This dates back to the earliest days of the colony when the first sailing ships were careened here (hulls cleaned and repainted).

The little park here, Harnett Park, is named for Richard Harnett senior, one of the earliest developers. He helped to get Mosman populated in the late 1800s. At the end of the bush path are twelve even concrete steps down to where a roadway is joined at the entrance to Mosman Rowing Club, where neatly dressed visitors are welcome to drop in for a quiet drink.

Now a choice. Continue along the road past the parking areas around the end of the bay, leaving Reid Park with its childrens playground. Follow the road to where it joins the main road to Mosman Junction (Avenue Road) then across to have a close look at Mosman's oldest building, The Barn. Otherwise —

An interesting alternative, although not for the handicapped, is to walk from the car park area straight into Reid Park, and keeping to the left, cross a path and head for a sealed footpath which leads up from the

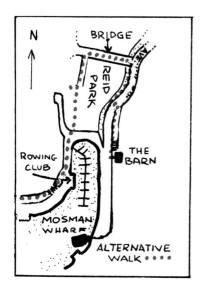

Sun dappled path on the way
to Old Cremorne Wharf

The last of the 'Ladies' leaving Old Cremorne

Ring Bolt Rock

Steel bridge at the end of Reid Park

The path above Ring Bolt Rock approaching
Corner Beach

The old path which leads to
the bridge

up from the park. before joining the path observe on the rock face to your left a metal plaque which reads:

> Bloxomes Landing
> This landing was originally on the waterfront and a
> path led from here to a Mr A Bloxome's 40 acres
> [16 hectares] estate and his mansion 'The Rangers', 1840.

This amazing house, only the second to be built in Mosman, had Elizabethan gables, a bell tower, turreted chimneys and a forty-two feet (13 metre) long flagged banqueting hall with exposed polished oak beams. It often housed famous people of the day, and it lasted until 1914, when developers finally got their hands on it and had it demolished. Suburban cottages were built in its place.

Now walk up the rather narrow path which is built on the original track up to 'The Rangers'. Turn right at the top and proceed over a beautiful steel footbridge to Avenue Road at the other end. Wander down to your right past the cabbage tree palms and half way around the first curve where trams once squealed their way to the wharf, cross the road and walk up the narrow road which leads to a flight of stairs and probably the best view of the pretty end of Mosman Bay. At the bottom of the steps join our friends who came the other way. We are now at The Barn. A plaque reads as follows:

> Governor Darling made a land grant of four acres [1.6 hectares] each to John Bell and Archibald Mosman at the head of Greater Sirius Cove for the purpose of erecting a wharf and various premises to cater for the local whaling industry consisting of a stone wharf six hundred feet (183 metres) long and five stone buildings, including The Barn.

'The Barn' built by Archibald Mosman in 1831 for
use in his whaling business

The Barn is thought to be the oldest surviving building on the lower North Shore, and is probably the last maritime structure left in Sydney dating from the early colonial period.

Now cross back to the path and continue in the direction of Mosman Wharf, past the HMS *Sirius* memorial, to a small shop where light refreshments can be purchased; keep some scraps for the ducks which are often around the wharf.

Shop Hours

Weekdays	7.00 a.m. to 8.00 p.m.
Saturday	7.30 a.m. to 6.30 p.m.
Sunday	7.30 a.m. to 6.00 p.m.

To the left, at the entrance to the wharf, are public toilets.

So ends trip number one. All that remains to do now is to catch the ferry back to Circular Quay, or if the legs are willing, Trip number two starts right here . . . Now read on.

Site of Mosman's Whaling Station

Mosman Wharf to
Taronga Zoo Wharf

Where Aborigines dined and trams once flew

Type of Terrain

The first part of this walk is up steep hills to the top of the ridge at Raglan Street, after which it's down hills and stairs to Sirius Cove, almost all of which is on pavement. The second half is not paved. Although the bush tracks are mostly in good condition some sections are

Third time ... unlucky

rough and stony, and after heavy rain some parts stay boggy for a few days. So it's not a walk for the very young, very old or handicapped.

Degree of Difficulty 5/10

Summary (with notes on wildlife and the dreaded tick)
This is a walk of contrast, from built-up areas to native bush, where, depending on luck, the time of day or season, one could expect to see any of the following: sulphur crested cockatoo, magpie, butcher bird, kingfisher, white ibis, heron (crane), silver gull, crested tern, various cormorants, fairy penguin, the silver flash of feeding whiting or the slow torpedo-shaped mullet, little lizards (skinks), big blue-tongue lizards, spiny anteaters and the common small goanna or water dragon, which leaps unexpectedly off logs and rocks, scattering leaves as it races into the bush.

Please avoid the black and dusky red hopping ants which can inflict a painful sting. Rubbing with the broken, hairy stem of bracken (a fern) is supposed to ease the pain. Snakes on or near the main tracks are extremely rare, but don't just blaze off into the mulga. Apart from frightening a snake, small shrubs and flowers are easily destroyed and in the sandy soil erosion quickly starts. Also during spring and into summer, tiny (about the size of a full stop) grass or seed larval ticks abound, and barging into the bush at this time may reward you with dozens of these little blokes who cause itching (often in the most sensitive parts) which can be most irritating. So as soon as possible remove the offenders with tweezers (some say dab the area first with turpentine), then apply an antiseptic with some sort of anti-itch additive. Later in the year you may pick up the odd larger tick, about three millimetres in size. Treat as above. (There is a rare disease known as Queensland tick typhus, so if symptoms such as fever, neck stiffness or joint and muscle pain develop, see a doctor without delay.)

Time
Allow approximately one hour.

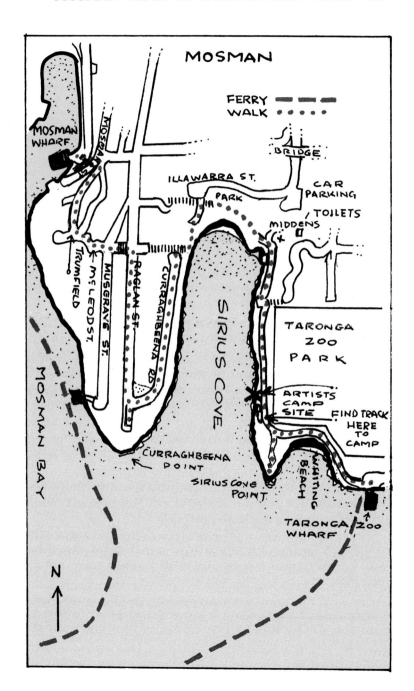

Clothes

A hat, strong footwear and perhaps a swimming costume and towel as, although the shark-proof net has been removed, Sirius Cove is a great place to cool off and there is a shower at the eastern end of the park in the toilet block.

Ferry Departure Details

Cremorne–Mosman ferries run approximately every half hour on weekdays and Saturdays, and hourly on Sundays.

Zoo ferries leave Circular Quay at approximately half-hour intervals on Saturdays and public holidays. They go directly to the Zoo wharf, from which the last ferry leaves at 7.00 p.m. (6.37 p.m. Sundays).

If in doubt, check at the ferry information kiosk (opposite jetty No. 4) or ring the number listed in the current telephone book.

The Walk

After a pleasant journey by ferry down quiet Mosman Bay we leave the Mosman wharf, and join the walkers from Trip 1, and head up the stairs opposite the wharf entrance. Cross the road at the top of the stairs and proceed up the footpath on the right, which takes us up Mosman Street and Trumfield Lane to winding, steep little McLeod Street. Cross Musgrave Street, go past the car park area to Raglan Street and turn right. Walk on down and across the road at the park.

Walk to the end of Raglan Street for city and harbour views (somewhat overgrown) before returning past the tower block.

What a shame building laws of a few years ago allowed huge home units to be built on land such as this, blocking the view and creating shade for the surrounding houses and public.

Let's move on around the corner and down Curraghbeena Road to its end, then turn right down paths and stairs, while glimpsing a bobbing orchestra of boats in the bay below. Proceed along a roughish and sometimes overgrown small section of bush track in front of some houses until you reach some concrete steps which lead to Sirius Cove reserve.

Often packed with people on Sundays, it's usually almost deserted

View towards Garden Island over Cremorne Point. The stone building with the columns was a guest house, 'Britanic Mansions', which has now been converted to home units

Going to the Zoo, Zoo, Zoo. Across Sirius Cove a ferry approaches the Zoo (Athol) Wharf

Sirius Cove Reserve, a pleasant picnic spot

on weekdays. This charming little park with its swings, adventure play-ground, drinking bubblers, toilets, showers and sandy beach was reclaimed over a period of about twenty years. However, evidence of human existence here dates back probably thousands of years.

To find it go to the south-eastern side of the park and find a narrow track beside the largest Port Jackson fig tree. Where this track joins a wider one a few metres away, look for the remains of an Aboriginal midden, one of several in the area. It was hereabouts that the original inhabitants squatted around eating their seafood meal, long before Jesus sat down to his Last Supper.

Shells half buried in a midden by the bush track above Sirius Cove

A water dragon hides in the shadows. This little goanna is commonly seen on Sydney waterfront bush tracks

Follow this sealed bush track south through a grove of paperbarks (melaleuca) past a little sandy beach (handy for a quick dip at low tide) and the green Sea Scout shed below (lst Clifton Gardens). Fur-ther on go up a short flight of stairs to a path, ignoring the steps up to Rickard Avenue beside the Zoo wall.

This track often becomes overgrown in summer, necessitating a sin-gle file in places, and during winter has wet patches after heavy rain. Three quarters of the way along the straight section before a curve, look down a rough narrow track towards the water. This is the sight of the old artists' camp. The easiest access is gained by continuing on until the track divides at the bend of the wall. Take the westerly point-ing track through the bush, which will lead down back to the camp site. It was in this area, back in 1889-90, that painters Tom Roberts, Arthur Streeton, Charles Conder and others lived in a little community known

From the bush track not far from the site of the Artists' Camp

as Curlew Camp. They had a small jetty, a boat, and on weekends friends could row over from one of the ferry wharves to enjoy the delights of the bush with them (no Lantana or Wandering Jew in those days) the sun, water, words and no doubt a bottle or two of wine—what a life it must have been!

Back in reality, keep on by the Zoo wall until it turns left, where a short five-minute detour can be made, if you don't mind bending and scraping around the rampant Lantana (introduced into Queensland in 1917 and still spreading) and Port Jackson fig to Sirius Point. Here you will find almost 360 degree views of Sydney, the Harbour, Cremorne, Mosman, and below the headland is a natural rock map of Australia, complete with rough state divisions.

Now back to the main track. Carry on, crossing a couple of little bridges and steep tracks down to Whiting Beach and on until the track turns south and later drops down to the right. Follow the solid stone stairs close to the water's edge, where several trams plunged into the Harbour.

The Athol Wharf tramline opened for service on 27 October 1917 and was closed in 1958 along with the rest of the North Sydney system. Its main claim to fame is that three times, in 1942, 1952 and 1958, trams ran out of control when fallen leaves and slush made the rails so slippery the wheels couldn't grip, despite sand being dropped on the rails. They hurtled past the entrance to the wharf, crashed through various buffers, flew off the embankment and into the Harbour, fortunately without loss of life.

Now to finish this walk just wander around the edge of the road and onto the Zoo wharf for the ferry ride back to the Quay, unless of course you'd like to carry on walking. If so, quickly use the conveniences on the wharf, such as toilets, telephones, bubblers, etc. and turn to Trip 3.

Stone stairs above the rocks near Whiting Beach

The wreckage of the Greycliffe

Taronga Zoo Wharf to Bradleys Head, the Zoo and Clifton Gardens

Hear the lions roar louder?
Then we'd better walk round to Chowder!

Note
This trip is divided into parts A, B and C to allow three walks of varying lengths, combined with a visit to the Zoo. This is a National Park, so no dogs allowed.

Type of Terrain
Part A is mostly a good quality wide walking track, usually well

'...with one of the finest dance pavilions in the southern hemisphere.'

maintained, not steep, with about forty or fifty steps scattered through-out, plus about the same number if you decide to visit the cannons.

Part B is similar, although the track gets a bit narrower in places.

Part C has a bit of everything. The track is mostly good, though there are narrow sections with rock steps of varying height, none of which should worry the average walker. Most of the last part is on footpath, although a reprieve is available on weekdays (working days) when a bus operates from Clifton Gardens to Bradleys Head Road, where one can catch another bus down to the wharf.

Degree of Difficulty 5/10

Summary

This is one of the best walks in Sydney for general Harbour views and native bush. Wide tracks, suitable for almost anyone with suit-able footwear, lead from the wharf through bush and parkland, past interesting naval and military sites above coves and bays with spec-tacular water views. The first part (A) is the easiest, the rest a little harder, owing to the extra time and distance involved. After leaving Clifton Gardens, the section after Kardinia Road is level, and from the Zoo, all downhill to the wharf.

Clothes

Hat, strong shoes, swimming costume for Clifton pool and sunscreen.

A catamaran type ferry approaches Taronga Zoo Wharf

Time

A.   One hour at least (plus 15 minutes to Zoo Gates or ferry)

B.   Half an hour easily (plus 15 minutes to Zoo Gates)

C.   One hour at least

A,B,C   Approximately three hours

Ferry Departure Details

On weekdays, Saturdays and public holidays ferries leave Circular Quay at approximately half-hour intervals. The boat goes directly to the Zoo wharf, from where the last ferry leaves at 7.00 p.m. (6.37 p.m. Sundays). Ferries don't necessarily leave from the same jetties on weekends as they do on weekdays, or run to the same timetables, so it is always best to check with the Ferry Information Kiosk (opposite No. 4 Jetty) or ring ferry information number in the current telephone book if you are in any doubt as to departure times, jetties or destinations.

Bus Information

Route 235 from Clifton Gardens, weekdays only, 7.30, 8.26, 8.54, 9.40, 10.40, 11.40 a.m. then none till 2.33, 3.44 and 4.14 p.m. Route 238 to Athol (Zoo) Wharf from Bradleys Head Road every 30 minutes. Route 250 to Lane Cove every 30 minutes.

The Walk

Having arrived at the Zoo wharf and walked up the ramp to the road, turn right up the footpath. At the pedestrian crossing keep to the path by the wire fence, built as a viewing area for a planned seal enclosure which has now been cancelled. At the end of the fenced path take the bush track that runs parallel to the road. Notice the old fake wood cement railing which was typical of the Zoo and surrounding park furniture and buildings.

On we go, up a few steps past a Sydney Harbour National Park sign, reminding us that we're in a bird and animal sanctuary, so no dogs allowed. This area, from here to Taylor's Bay, is also known as Ashton Park, named after the Hon. James Ashton, MLC, a prominent citizen of early this century. Sudden sounds of something rushing

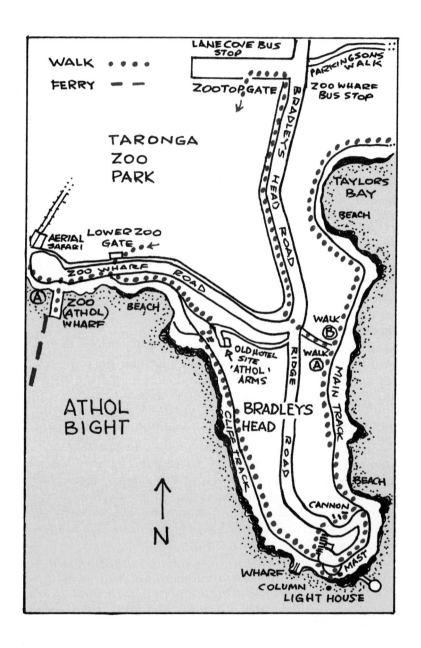

Restored old building in what was the main picnic area of Ashton Park

"SYDNEY HARBOUR NATIONAL PARK. ALL FLORA AND FAUNA PROTECTED. DOGS AND LITTERING PROHIBITED. GAS FIRES ONLY. NO CAMPING."

Angophoras offer shade on the way to Bradleys Head

A reasonably unspoiled bush track a few kilometres from Australia's biggest city

about in the bush will turn out to be water dragon goannas, very common on this walk. They are easy to see as they tend to sit very still until the last moment before leaping off down a slope, scattering leaves and twigs as they race away.

Along this first part of the track just after the park sign is a good grove of pittosporum trees (the leaves have wart like marks) which makes a trip through here in late August–early September, when they flower, a perfumed delight. On the right hand side a little further along is a park type seat on a sandstone rock, and typical of the old style resters scattered throughout these walks. With the recent infiltration of exotic plants, many of these seats now just stare blindly into dense bush.

Go down a few steps over a little bridge and on the left in the bush there are several large spiky plants, often patterned with children's initials and general comments on life.

Where the path divides, take the uppermost to the slippery-slide, prettily placed near a little stone amphitheatre. At the top of the grassy picnic area is a charming old weatherboard building recently restored, part hall, part ranger's house, which dates back to the 1860s when this area contained a pavilion, a hotel (the 'Athol Arms'), kiosks, picnic grounds (toilets at rear). Looking west from the steps of the pavilion is peaceful Athol Bight, where out in the middle the famous Cunard *Queens* anchored during the last war while waiting to embark up to 5000 troops.

Now take the central path back down to join our original track at a four-way intersection. The choice here is to continue down to Athol Beach, usually partly covered in rubbish blown in by prevailing westerlies, or carry on towards Bradleys Head. All this area around here was owned by Sydney Ferries Limited, which ran a regular service to a wharf below where there is now a crumbling wall. In those days (the Athol service commenced in 1905) masses of people would file up to the park with its large razzle dazzle or roundabout, swings, see saws etc., and all around were little wooden picnic kiosks where families could shelter from the elements at lunch time. Having explored, carry on towards Bradleys Head, by the main track which heads in a southerly direction.

As we proceed notice how in the westerly aspect native plants flourish and exotics die back in the dry heat and sunlight. We come to an area where a really superb vista of the Harbour opens up, before we wander up lots of well spaced steps through a beautiful

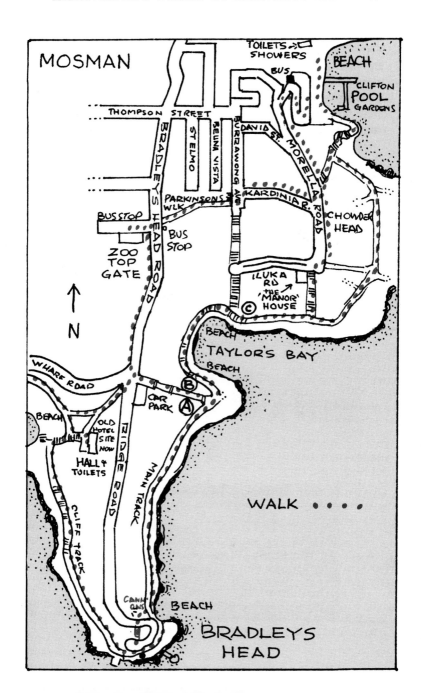

stand of angophoras. At the top of the climb, glimpsed through the greenery, is the archetypical Sydney tourist 'photo opportunity'. (Until recently the Navy moored its redundant ships below here.)

As we round the first part of the headland we pass under coral and brush box trees, before looking over a charming, shaped stone wharf, originally used to transport equipment for the fortifications.

Bradleys Head was named for Lieutenant William Bradley, who with Captain Hunter landed here late in January 1788. The Aboriginal name for this area is Burrogy.

The mast or fighting top on the headland belonged to HMAS *Sydney*. She was a light cruiser that took part in the first Australian naval engagement of the First World War against the German Cruiser SMS *Emden,* near Cocos Island on 9 November 1914. An interesting memorial to the four 'Sydneys' is by the car park.

On the rock below is a stone column from the old Sydney Post Office which is used to measure one nautical mile from the tower on Fort Denison. Around to the east is a sister lighthouse to the one on Cremorne Point.

Bradleys Head, showing the Lighthouse, *Sydney's* mast and the doric column from the General Post Office

Fortifications from 1871 at Bradleys Head

Bradleys Head is the best easily accessible point in Sydney from which to watch the Harbour's various shipping and boating activities. Indeed, shocked spectators have witnessed two disasters near here this century. The first was in November 1927 when the Sydney Ferry *Greycliffe*, with about 125 passengers, including children returning from school, was run down in mid harbour between Garden Island and Bradleys Head by the Union Steamship Company's 7585-ton *Tahiti*. Forty-two people died.

Just over ten years later, on 13 February 1938, the little ferry Rodney sank while carrying 100 passengers, mostly teenage girls who wanted a last chance to wave goodbye to the sailors on the US Navy's cruiser *Louisville* which was leaving Sydney after a short stay. Just after Garden Island, Rodney changed course and the crowd on the open top deck quickly changed sides. The sudden shift of weight was too much, and the ferry rolled over and sank. Nineteen people drowned in the tragedy.

For those not wanting to see the old cannon, continue on around the roadway as far as the 'Gas Fires Only' sign by a flight of stairs. The rest who want to see the guns and beautifully made stone emplacements go up the stairs alongside the toilets and at the top, over the road, aiming menacingly at the trees, are the weapons of last century.

The military started to build the fortress, down below, near the Sydney's mast in 1841, but apart from a gun pit and a stone wall, nothing more was done until 1871 when three gun pits, a stone gallery for riflemen and an underground powder magazine were built. None of these have ever been used in anger.

Having seen all there is to see, go to the eastern side of the clearing, find the stairs and follow these to the roadway below. Then walk to the hairpin bend where the other walkers are waiting.

Swimmers, picnickers and fossickers: find the stairs by the 'Gas Fires Only' sign, walk down to the little sandy beach with its rock pools at lowish tide. This is a good spot in winter as the southerlies can't reach you.

The rest of us can examine the typical Ashton Park shelter shed before continuing along the track which is mostly shady, breezy and often cool after lunchtime, even on summer days.

Along the track you pass open views towards the Heads, past ferny bracken and the somewhat mysterious die back of the angophoras and eucalypts, up some rock stairs and along until we reach a good track which leads us to the left. This then is the end of Part A. Therefore, those wishing to catch a ferry or those who want to visit the Zoo just walk up the track to the left as far as the roadway, and either go down the roadway or (more enjoyable) down the pathway opposite through the picnic area and back around the track to the wharf. Zoo visitors will turn right at the top of the track and walk up the main road till they reach the main gates at the top of the hill, taking care to avoid the traffic, as there is no footpath.

The rest of us can start on Part B by carrying on and enjoying this quiet stretch of track which leads around Taylor's Bay, named after Lieutenant James Taylor of 1810. Soon you will come to some steps.

Looking towards Rose Bay over Taylors Bay

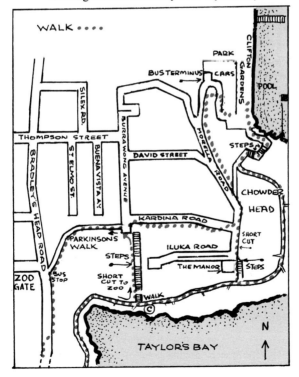

climb these and pass through a miniature rainforest, then down some more stone stairs. Soon on the left is the lower extremity of a large house, as evidenced by the overgrown rock wall, and then a white house, and a Sydney Harbour National Park signpost — civilisation has been reached, and with it the end of part B. So those who want to visit the Zoo or have a ferry to catch, just follow the many stairs up as far as they go, then cross the road to Parkinson's Walk and continue straight on. Just past some willows the path veers left and soon reaches the Zoo top gates and the Zoo (Athol) Wharf bus stop.

Those of us left on the main walk (Part C), carry on along the track, (or you can follow the little track down to Taylor's Bay with its beach and pleasant walkable rocks). This track often gets rather overgrown.

So we wind our way through patches of cultivated bush, sometimes under the watchful eyes of binoculars in the houses above. Tracks lead off here and there to the rocky waterfront below, but we keep on and now we're in one of the best heeled areas of Mosman, known as Clifton Gardens. Undaunted, we push on until we reach the last house 'The Manor', which is the largest in Mosman.

Built before the turn of the century, this amazing building was known originally as 'Bakewell's Folly', after the name of its builder. It was purchased by the Theosophical Society who established Radio Station 2GB here, the GB initials standing for Giordano Bruno, the sixteenth century Italian philosopher, inspirer of the Theosophists.

'The Manor', original home of radio station 2GB

If it's a hot day and a shorter walk to Clifton Gardens is called for, then walk up the stairs alongside 'The Manor', up the short but steep part of Morella Road, then down the other side until a pathway leads off down to the right. Follow this to the picnic grounds and swimming pool.

Otherwise push on around the sometimes overgrown, rocky and wet track for several hundred metres, before turning left at a triangle of tracks (perhaps the partly obscured signposts will show the way). A short distance further on, take the right fork then head north up through rocks and past another crossroads—go straight on—and soon the path opens up onto a grass area, leading to another footpath. A large part of the bush we've travelled through has been carefully restored from the ravages of fire and exotic invasion by a keen local group of enthusiasts. Two of the original members were the late Bradley sisters, whose method of controlling the infiltration of imported plants and weeds has been used as a model and taken up by numerous councils and government bodies.

Follow the footpath and stairs down the hill to Clifton Gardens swimming enclosure and reserve. Here you will find showers, toilets and tables, and a large area in the middle of the grass where once stood a huge dance pavilion, 'one of the finest in the southern hemisphere, with a floor measuring 225 feet by 40 feet [69 by 12 metres]. 1200 dancers or 2000 seated for concerts could be accommodated'. Nearby at the water's edge was a circular double-decked swimming enclosure.

Ever since early last century this cove has been known as Chowder Bay, after the seafood dish prepared by American whalers who anchored in the bay. Indeed, in 1832 one of them, a Captain Cliffe, bought 15 acres (6 hectares) of the then government gardens and erected a house which he called 'Cliffeton'.

When the first hotel was built there in 1871 it was called the Clifton Arms and soon the area became known as Clifton Gardens. Some years later David Thompson built of stone the magnificent three storey 'Marine Hotel'.

About 1905 Sydney Ferries Limited bought the hotel and grounds, running its steamers there packed with picnickers. The hotel changed

Clifton Gardens Reserve

Down the stairs to Chowder Bay

hands several times over the years, but in 1966 mounting pressure from conservative locals helped close its doors. The following year one of Sydney's rare and attractive waterfront hotel buildings was demolished.

Facilities at Clifton Gardens include showers, changing sheds, toilets, taps, tables, sharkproof swimming pool and plenty of shade, which is no doubt why this place is usually packed on summer Sundays, often with large family and organised picnic groups.

The magnificent 'Cliffo'

Time to go, so take the stairs by the telephone box at the south-western corner of the park, then wander up the road a short distance and take the pathway through the little park on the site of the hotel. Where the park comes back to the road (and providing it's a working day) look to the right for the bus stop. The bus (Route 235) will take you up to Bradleys Head Road from where you can catch a bus (Route 238) to the Zoo (Athol) wharf or walk downhill to the wharf.

For the remaining walkers we'll just continue up Morella Road, noting across the bay the interesting group of buildings belonging to the Army marine school, until we reach Kardinia Road, following it past many grand houses to its end, where you turn left down a short hill (Burrawong Avenue) and cross the road to Parkinson's Walk.

The rest is easy, just proceed straight along until some coral trees where the track veers left until the Zoo is seen. Catch buses here to the wharf or Lane Cove (Route 250), or just walk on down the winding road to the ferry, avoiding any traffic on the way. Don't forget, last ferry at 6.37 p.m. Sundays, Good Fridays, Christmas Days, and 7.00 p.m. weekdays, Saturdays and public holidays

As you sail away from the wharf remember the old children's riddle—Why did Cre-morne?—Because it saw Athol Bight off Bradleys Head!

Taronga Zoo top gates

Athol (Zoo) Wharf to Spit Bridge, via Balmoral

For young oldies or old youngies

Hop around the rock!

Type of Terrain
Almost all on waterfront rocks with some sand and at high tide, wet feet. Links up with the following trip for hours of fresh air and exercise. In fact more of a rock hop than a walk.

Degree of Difficulty 9/10

Summary
Bus from the wharf, walk along Balmoral Esplanade, then around rocks to Chinaman's Beach, and after that more rock-hopping to The Spit. Catch a bus to city or wharf, or alternatively walk on *(see Trip 5)*.

Time
Roughly one hour.

Clothes
Hat, good synthetic-soled shoes (joggers etc.), perhaps a swimming costume and of course sunscreen.

Ferry Departure Details
Full details Trip 3.

Bus Details
Balmoral Beach bus leaves Athol (Zoo) Wharf after meeting the ferry. Wynyard buses from The Spit every ten or fifteen minutes. Manly Wharf buses from The Spit approximately every fifteen minutes.

The Walk
Leave the ferry at Taronga Zoo Wharf and catch Balmoral Beach Bus Route 238 at the top of the ramp. As you weave in and out of the back streets of Mosman imagine the days when trams made a similar journey, except that they ran on reserved track in the final stage, winding through bushland with the ground often covered in a carpet of railway daisies (coreopsis), then through a rock cutting and

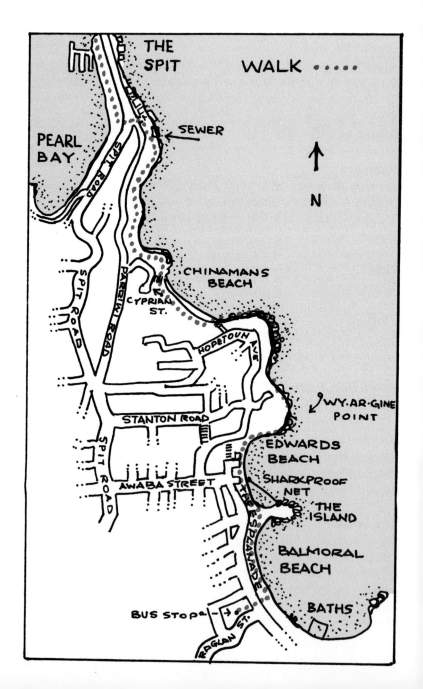

suddenly out to the brilliant blue waters of Hunter Bay. It was the perfect way of arriving at sparkling Balmoral (named after Queen Victoria's Scottish castle). As we're in a bus we'll get off at the bottom of Raglan Street, cross the Esplanade and walk north towards the Island. Along this stretch of beach one can swim, hire a boardsailer, picnic, use the shops (food, drink, bottle shop) as well as the usual toilets, taps, showers etc.

Near the Island with its nice little bridge, notice the band rotunda (built by Mosman Council as a depression project) and nearby the Pavilion, which houses a restaurant.

Just above the last grassed area is a little bush lookout, formed in honour of local historian and ex-mayor Jack Carroll, whose invaluable collection of photographs are on view at Mosman Library. Now continue from the grassed area onto the beach.

Just past the lookout is a large block of flats where once stood an unusual Roman type amphitheatre, built in 1924 in the hope that a new Messiah would appear and come and teach there. An Indian, Krishnamurti, was believed by many, especially the Theosophical Society, to be the one, so a Star of India Congress was held in 1925 at the amphitheatre. Krishnamurti stayed at The Manor, mentioned in Trip 3. However, by 1939 enthusiasm had waned to the extent that the amphitheatre was sold. It was demolished and the very ordinary building we see today built in its place.

Continue on from Edwards Beach (the stretch from the Island north to the rocks) around to the point (Wy-ar-gine) with its delightful

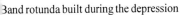

Band rotunda built during the depression

The Esplanade, Balmoral Beach

Rock pool with a view. Wy-ar-gine Point

natural rock pool known locally as 'The Frazz', then on around the rocks, some of which are beautifully eroded by wind and water.

The weekday I made the trip I came across two minor obstacles: high tide, which meant sandshoes off in a couple of places; and several groups of naked gentlemen taking the sun on the rocks. Perhaps they belonged to some sort of club, as there seemed to be plenty of members!

After rounding a headland find your way in front of some boatsheds and front lawns to Chinamans Beach. Hereabouts artist Ken Done lived and gained much inspiration for his colourful paintings.

In the 1870s this area was a pleasure ground known as 'Rosherville', after a house that stood here. Later it became the site of Chinese market gardens and although long shells known as Chinese fingernails are found here, it seems the name came from the oriental farmers of the vegetable gardens.

To really understand what this enchanting part of Sydney was like before the Volvo and BMW set arrived, one should read Nancy Phelan's delightful childhood reminiscences in her book *A Kingdom by the Sea.*

After the beach there are several houses, all of which provide a little path around their property to assist the high tide walker—with one exception, at that house one has to walk up and through the lower yard to regain the rocks.

Chinamans Beach and Rosherville Park

Cool path on a hot day

Middle Harbour waterfront house
with Lighthouse above

As you wander along the shore of Shell Cove you'll eventually come to some boulders strewn about, mostly covered by bushes. These date back to the building of the tram line above in Parriwi Road which was extended to The Spit in 1900 and was in use for 58 years.

Continue along the rocks and sand popular with mid-week sun-bathers until the large, grim-looking concrete sewerage building is reached. It was above here somewhere that in April 1877 Mr L'Estrange crossed Middle Harbour on a tightrope before a crowd of well over eight thousand, packed into 21 ferries, tugs, etc. Brass bands played, food and drink was consumed, and at four o'clock out strode the gentleman himself, 346 feet (106 metres) above the water and 1420 feet (437 metres) to go!

Off he went and after a short distance he stood on one leg, sat down, waved, then lay flat out along the rope, and generally enter-tained the mob below with a dazzling display. The rest was almost easy after that and he finished in fine style. For his efforts L'Estrange was given a memento in the form of a six-pointed star with a draw-ing of The Spit and Clontarf, in the centre of which was a one and a quarter carat diamond and a purse with sovereigns and six American twenty dollar pieces. Not bad for a short afternoon stroll ! (It's now believed that this event took place across Willoughby Bay).

From the sewerage building continue on behind the Middle Har-bour Yacht Club, once occupied by The Spit Swimming Baths, where over the years tens of thousands of school children poured out of special trams and ran in for a dive, a swim, and probably a push and a ducking.

That's about it for this trip. Manly Wharf bus passengers and walkers who are continuing, cross at the traffic lights, and Wynyard (city) passengers head straight on past the sixteen foot Skiff Club to the bus stop. An alternative for those who are continuing is to also go straight on without crossing the road, but to cross under the bridge. The Manly Wharf bus (route 144) passes about every fifteen min-utes. Manly ferry details and directions on how to walk to Manly are listed in Trip 5.

See you there.

Spit Bridge around the Waterfront to Manly Wharf

Where the duke faced hazard, and a beach disappears

Type of Terrain

This used to be a rugged walk, with rock hopping and bush bashing, but since the extensive improvements to the tracks it is now a much easier trip. So thanks to Manly Council and National Parks for such splendid work. However, there are still a few rough sections, with numerous steps, stairs, steep inclines and large rocky areas.

Clickity Click . . . . Clickity Clack

Summary

After leaving the waterfront at The Spit we walk around bush tracks until we reach Sandy Bay. From there we cross the sand or use the grass verge. At the end of Clontarf we use bush paths again and unless we want to rock hop we stay on them for the duration of the walk.

Degree of Difficulty 6/10

Time

Roughly half a day.

Ferry Departure Details

Ferries leave approximately every thirty minutes, jetcats every twenty. Last trip from Manly Wharf 12.10 a.m. weekdays and Saturdays, 11.25 p.m. Sundays.

Ferries take about 35 minutes for the journey, jetcats about fifteen. Special timetables operate on public holidays, and as all timetables are open to change its best to check at the ferry information kiosk, or ring the ferry information number in the current telephone book.

Bus Departure Details

Buses leave Manly Wharf for St Leonards Station (Route 144) via The Spit every fifteen minutes. Buses from Wynyard via The Spit leave every few minutes. Enquire at Wynyard or Manly terminus.

Clothes

I suggest people with sensitive skin should wear long trousers as the track may be overgrown in places with spiky native plants. In summer a hat would be good, as this is a long walk. Also walking shoes like sandshoes, sneakers, joggers, even boots would be a sensible idea, as would sunscreen and a swimming costume.

Season

Please read the second part of the summary for Trip 2, particularly the section referring to ticks. However, since the tracks have been remade, ticks are not such a problem.

The Walk

The Aborigines knew The Spit as Burra Bra, and the Clontarf area as Warringa. The Europeans named Clontarf after the picnic grounds of the same name near Dublin, Ireland, and the Australian version was considered the most shady pleasure grounds in Sydney.

So having arrived at The Spit either by walking around from Balmoral or by bus from Wynyard or Manly, we set off over the bridge in a northerly direction, finding some stairs at the end to our left. Descending these we then cross under the bridge with its traffic roar, noticing the old punt ramp at the water's edge and the historical monument to our left at the bottom of the steep little road.

The old punt runt ramp and remains of tramline

The road just above us used to be the approach road for the old Spit Bridge. On 31 May 1949 onlookers were horrified to see an Albion double-decker bus smash through the fence railings and crash into the ground metres below. Four people died. The driver had been unable to straighten the bus after rounding a curve.

The punt ramp is probably close to the spot where a local resident, a Mr Peter Ellery, started a hand punt service in 1850. The government took over in 1888, adding a steam vessel the following year, to link up with a horse-drawn coach which ran to Manly three times a day.

In 1900 the electric tram reached The Spit from Spit Junction and eleven years later the service from The Spit to Manly opened. By 1924 passengers could leave the Spit tram, cross over the new bridge and join trams about where we're standing, for the first time.

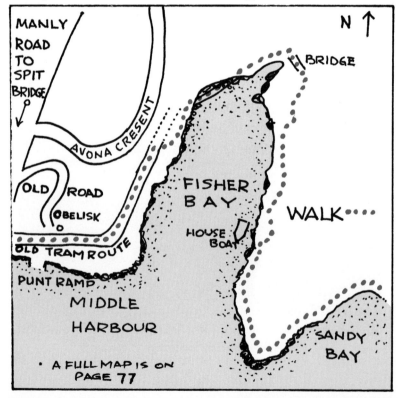

Middle Harbour and the Spit Bridge

The last part of this tramline must have been magnificent, dropping as it did from high up at Balgowlah, round through bushland, with great views of the tranquil waters of Middle Harbour and its bays and hills, until its end here, with a rock face on one side and waterfront on the other. It seems not enough people appreciated it, however, for the Manly tram system closed in 1939. The present opening bridge was finished in 1958.

Let's head off east along the path that was once a tramline, until rounding a corner we come to the end of what used to be the rail ballast. (The track from here to Castle Rock was completed by workmen from Manly Council, and a great job they've done. So too have the National Parks and Wildlife Service who are responsible for the excellent work from Castle Rock to Forty Baskets Beach.)

Turn right down stone steps and take the left fork and come out under an overhanging rock at the end of the bay. (Could be a good spot to catch whiting.) At half tide or so, herons (or cranes) are often seen wading about, stabbing at fish here and there, while silver gulls cry and preen.

Follow the wooden pathway over the sand at the back of the bay and behind a grove of trees. (At least we'll miss seeing some of the rubbish blown in by southerly winds.) In the corner we'll cross over the bridge and continue on past privet and other exotics and an old

Peaceful Fisher Bay

houseboat which is occupied (private property). Now around the point with its lookout seat and views of the Spit and Middle Harbour, then east past colourful moss-covered rocks until, above the beach, take the right fork down to the waterfront.

Sandy Bay dries at low tide like a British cove, leaving boats lying about on the sand. Wander on, enjoying the mostly clean white sand, past the boatshed, to Clontarf Reserve and the swimming pool, shower and toilet block, shop and barbecue area.

Low tide, Sandy Bay

Royalty visited Clontarf on 12 March 1868 when Queen Victoria's second son, the Duke of Edinburgh, came to a fund-raising picnic here, held in his honour. Also present among the large crowd was a well dressed Irish gentleman who was about to become as well known as the Duke himself.

Clontarf, where a Duke was shot

Events were running smoothly when suddenly the 'gentleman' ran at His Royal Highness, whipped out a revolver and fired off two shots. One hit the Duke in the arm, the other hitting a bystander's foot! The royal arm was, however, only slightly injured and was soon fully recovered. The Irishman, Henry James O'Farrell, was not so lucky. After being almost lynched by the wild crowd he was tried and convicted. O'Farrell's protest against the treatment of his coun trymen by the English was soon to be over. Having been found guilty of 'shooting at, with intent to murder, the Duke of Edinburgh' he was executed at Darlinghurst gaol on 21 April 1868.

We carry on now along the beach past the concrete sewer tower (on the southern side of which, behind a tree on the corner is a concrete tablet marking the site of the shooting). Continue now to the Corner Beach. During construction of the sewer, workmen could

Around the rocks from Castle Rock

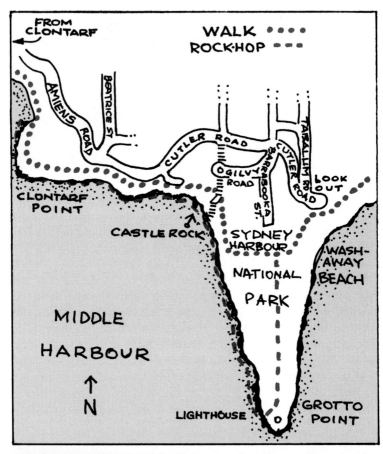

walk from one side of Middle Harbour to the other, under water, by
way of the pipeline.

At the top left hand side of the beach (there should be a sign),
follow a track and steps as they rise and continue around the point
past overhanging rocks, while below the white sand reflects through
the usually clear water. The path is full of variety as it rises and falls
along the edge of the land and the back yards of some houses. (Here
and there trails or steps lead down to little beaches along the way.
Ignore them if you can, unless of course you want to travel to Grotto

Native bush on Grotto Point

Lighthouse Grotto Point   Dobroyd Headland with Manly Beyond

by the waterfront. See map.) Just before Castle Rock the track rises suddenly in a 'Z' then crosses a bridge until it reaches the main cement footpath from Ogilvy Road to Castle Rock Beach.

Turn right down four small flights of stairs, then turn left into the bush along a trail. This wanders along and around about before rising up near a cave then over a wooden bridge. We then continue through bushland among rocky outcrops and angophoras as birds chirp and the sun belts down. Follow the path, stone stairs and wire fences until our path crosses another at the sign posts. Go south down along the ridge to Grotto Point or carry on in a generally north-easterly direction, according to your whim! (The Grotto track is rough.)

Here I assume those who rock hopped around the shore found their way to Grotto, climbed the short ladder, the stairs, and ended up at the lighthouse. So those who went on the south track to the same place can return with them and continue on with us, at the top of the path (of which there are two, both leading back to the main path).

From here as we stroll along the rising track, headlands, harbour and ocean are revealed, as ferries roll across the Heads and

Washaway Beach, Middle Head, South Head — New Zealand?

Over Middle Harbour to Balmoral, Mosman with the city beyond

ocean-bound ships nudge the first ocean swells. Views everywhere as we rise and fall behind the scrub. Below is Washaway Beach, so named because, mainly in winter, the action of the heavy seas drags away the sand leaving bare rock exposed. I think we can and will see enough from the track without branching off to the lookout. Soon the track swings around in a more northerly direction cross areas of rock from where one can properly appreciate the width of the Heads, which is approximately 1500 metres.

This is a great walk to do in winter, as the brilliance of the wattle trees along here can almost warm a cool, grey June day! Next, below the road, the track passes Crater Cove.

Clinging to the rocks can be seen small makeshift squatters' houses

Crater Cove with a small bombora breaking near Dobroyd Headland

There's a track winding back . . .

that have been perching there since the 1920s. They are private property, so don't trespass. Near the headland are three buoys which mark a dangerous bombora. This happens when, under certain weather conditions, waves suddenly rise and break over a shelf of rock. They did so in 1874 when Staff Commander John Gowland and Henry Peterson were drowned, and their survey boat swamped.

From here we stay on the path and follow the signs as we wander through typical coastal stunted bush of small eucalypts, banksias, she-oaks, etc. At an intersection turn right (the left fork goes up to Tania Park, which is mostly playing fields, with toilets and taps). Keep your eyes open around here for pretty striped skinks (small lizards) with reddish tails, also honey eaters as they bounce about seeking lunch.

Carry on down the main path, over the ridge, down steps through the scrub, until we reach another intersection and another choice. Straight on partly following the waterfront and passing through Reef Beach or, left for quite some distance through interesting changing bush, until a Reef Beach sign is reached at a 'T' intersection. Turn right here and wander down under the voluptuous arms of the angophoras, down the wooden steps until the track is reached at another 'T'. Right for Reef Beach, left to Forty Baskets for a sharkproof net and viewproof swimming costumes.* Also find toilets just a bit further on around the bush path past the usually closed kiosk. The track then leads on to, and climbs up past, boatsheds, to

* Until recently Reef Beach was 'Clothes Optional'

a sealed road named Gourlay Avenue. Just near the first houses on the right find a path which leads across the pretty little bridge. On the other side turn down North Harbour Street, formerly Lister Street, on which, just around the corner above the park is a very pleasant wooden house, and a bit further on a shop with drinks, food etc., which is open all weekend.

Now cross the park near the water's edge to the northern end and climb the stairs to King Avenue and a historical plaque under a Port Jackson fig. Wind up and around to Lauderdale Avenue. (Catch a bus from over the road to Manly Wharf if you wish — details in Trip 6.) Just past a few houses head off to the right away from the road, down a path to your right which will lead you all the way around the waterfront footpath past Fairlight Beach, pool and Oceanworld, to Manly Wharf. (Full information for this last section can be found in Trip 6.)

So that's it. Just catch a ferry now, sit down and enjoy the always interesting Sydney Harbour, without moving a leg!

Boats, North Harbour

Manly Wharf to Reef Beach

Where sharks swim with people and
people can swim with sharks

Type of Terrain

This is a walk anyone can do, although only the first half is possible for wheelchairs. Elderly people will find only gentle grades (the steepest being past the Art Gallery). Most of the walk is on footpath.

Summary

After leaving Manly Cove follow a footpath around the edge of North Harbour keeping water on one side and houses on the other. At about half way a bus can be caught back to the Manly Wharf. Otherwise carry on to a large open park, then through bush on a good track to

Freshwater in shallow water. Teething problems in 1983.

a swimming and picnic area at Forty Baskets. Return the way you came.

Degree of Difficulty 3/10

Time
A slow walking hour to the park, plus ten minutes to Forty Baskets reserve.

Ferry Details
Ferries leave approximately every thirty minutes, jetcats every twenty. Last trip from Manly Wharf 12.10 a.m. weekdays and Saturdays, 11.25 p.m. Sundays.

Ferries take about 35 minutes for the journey, jetcats about fifteen. Special timetables operate on public holidays, and as all timetables are open to change its best to check at the ferry information kiosk, or ring the ferry information number in the current telephone book.

Bus Details
Bus routes that serve Lauderdale Avenue are 132 and 171 every 30 minutes weekdays, every hour on weekends, approximately, but check at bus area outside Manly Wharf before setting out on the walk. The short walk direction can be reversed, by catching the bus first, then walking back from the King Avenue stop. Veer to your right just after King Avenue and follow the separate path back to the wharf.

Clothes
Hat, sensible footwear, swimming costume, sunscreen and perhaps a windcheater.

The Walk
Manly has many attractions at different times of the year and should you contemplate this easy walk during the long weekend in October

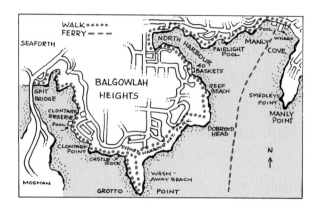

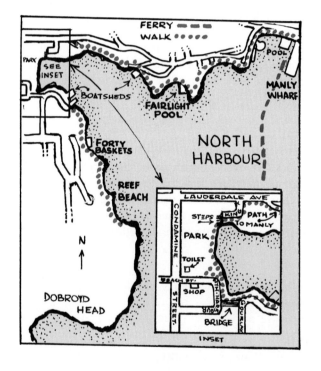

perhaps you could return in time to enjoy the Three Day Jazz Festival in the Corso amphitheatre.

Leave Manly Wharf and walk along to your left under the Norfolk Island pines and in front of the small netted swimming area where once people thronged to enjoy sun, sea and sand in the safety of the huge swimming baths which enclosed half the bay (details of which can be found at the end of Trip 7).

Where the pines finish look in at the Art Gallery and Museum. The Gallery is well worth a visit to see the good collection of mostly Australian paintings, ceramics and hand-blown glass. The main exhibition changes every three months. Hours are: Tuesday to Friday 10 a.m. to 4 p.m. Weekends and holidays 12 noon to 5 p.m. Closed Mondays, Christmas Day and Good Friday.

People with wheelchairs, children's strollers etc., should take the path up past the Gallery and follow it around to the left until it joins up with the steps from below. Others, more agile, can speed around corners inside a plastic tube at the Giant Waterworks Slides, or visit Oceanworld (10 a.m. to 5.30 p.m. seven days) to watch, at only arm's length away, sharks cruising slowly by with rows of teeth on standby.

Having studied the grace of fish movement, ours will take us towards the Harbour through archways (or up the stairs to the Manly Pier Restaurant, if time and dress permit) around the corner and up

Oceanworld, waterslides and Manly Art Gallery offer diversions on this walk

Close enough to touch.

Delwood Beach, pines and streamlined bush

the thirty or so steps to the path above.

Now the walk really starts. Just follow the footpath around to Fairlight Beach (about ten minutes' stroll). This delightful little strip of sand and its rock pool face roughly south, so it's a good place to swim and sunbake when 'black' nor'easters blow. Great too for snorkling around the rocks, or just messing about in the water. There are showers, taps and toilets nearby. And the view! This is one of the very few harbour beaches that look out to sea, and on a clear day New Zealand is not *quite* visible.

What could be seen from here in June 1949 was an old Dutch submarine, K.XII, which was under tow from Manly Wharf, where she had been on display. In a stiff southerly wind the lines parted from the tug and she drifted free, ending up hard aground on the western side of Fairlight Beach. She stayed there for about a year before being finally towed away for scrapping.

The stranded Dutch submarine K.XII

Fairlight Pool and Beach, without a submarine

Wind, the invisible conductor, The Esplanade, Fairlight

Carry on walking around the next headland with its views of the bay full of boats nosing into the wind, then along the footpath behind the boatshed to the little roadway which turns back into footpath again.

Near the end of the bay the pathway rises up and joins the main road, which is Lauderdale Avenue. Cross the road to catch the bus back to Manly Wharf if the legs have lost interest. Wheelchair and stroller pushers can also turn around and head back the way they came if they prefer, as ahead lie twenty or thirty steps into a park.

From Lauderdale Avenue turn left into King Avenue and follow it to its end where you will see a plaque under a Port Jackson fig. This informs us that 'nearby in 1788 Governor Phillip commenced his first overland exploration from Manly towards Pittwater. In 1822 the first road to Sydney via Pittwater and Gordon had its origin in this locality.' (Our thanks to Manly Historical Society, 1940 for this plaque.)

Take the path on the right which leads us down some steps and around into a pleasant green park. At the south-western corner are toilets, swings, etc. and in the street above, a shop with sweets, snacks, drinks and so on, which is open on weekends.

As you walk east up the little road look up to your right at the superb little timber cottage with its four cabbage tree palms and suddenly the past is present. The street (North Harbour) turns right; at its top find a path to your left that leads you over a pretty wooden

Timber and corrugated iron and cabbage tree palms

How to get from Gourlay Avenue to North Harbour Street

bridge into leafy Gourlay Street, where again turn left and follow the street through the bush of Wellings Reserve, down past the boatsheds where a dirt road follows on. At its end is Forty Baskets Reserve, with a swimming pool, slippery dip, toilets, tap and on weekends a shop. (One explanation for the name, Forty Baskets, is that that amount of fish was sent over to the Quarantine Station as a gift for the troops that had just returned from the Sudan.)

This then is as far as you can walk on good level ground; the first part of the way to Reef Beach is along the waterfront, perhaps getting your feet wet if the tide is high. Nevertheless, if you're hot and would like to swim without a shark net, wander around the track to Reef Beach and just dive in!

Sometimes strange characters loiter around the periphery of Reef Beach, so to avoid any unpleasantness stay on the main track, or the beach itself if you are unfamiliar with the area.

I suggest the most pleasant way back is simply to retrace your steps and enjoy the beautiful scenery at a different time of day.

Manly Wharf to Shelly Beach

Where gasworks worked and the first surfers surfed

Type of Terrain

The full walk is mostly over pavement footpaths and stairs, with a middle section which has roughish short tracks, some beach sand and rock steps. This section can be left out if desired, taking a fairly long uphill walk instead.

So it's a walk for the reasonably fit and not for the handicapped.

Degree of Difficulty 5/10

Summary

This time we start off walking along suburban footpaths around the harbour and then into some bush, across a beach and up a winding bush road. We come out at the top and then wander on down footpaths to the splendid ocean front along a marine walkway to another beach. We then walk around a small headland with native bush, a good path and sweeping views of land and sea. Finally back to Manly Beach, the shops and a seat on a return ferry.

A surfboat 'shoots' the 'breakers'.

Time
Allow at least two and a half hours

Clothes
Hat, good walking shoes, swimming costume and of course sunscreen. See Trip 2 for reference to ticks.

Ferry Departure Details
Ferries leave approximately every thirty minutes, jetcats every twenty. Last trip from Manly Wharf 12.10 a.m. weekdays and Saturdays, 11.25 p.m. Sundays.

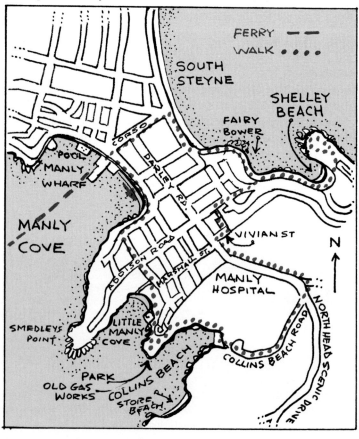

Ferries take about 35 minutes for the journey, jetcats about fifteen. Special timetables operate on public holidays, and as all timetables are open to change its best to check at the ferry information kiosk, or ring the ferry information number in the current telephone book.

The ferry *Collaroy* approaching Manly Wharf, as lesser craft ignore her

The Walk

Well, here we are in the first named place in Sydney Harbour, Manly. Governor Phillip wrote of the local Aborigines that 'their confidence and manly behaviour made me give the name of Manly Cove to this place'.

We leave the modernised Manly Wharf with all its food and amusements by the first exit to our right. Then walk along the waterfront around the cove with its collection of well kept cabin launches. Follow the curve of the path, taking the first pathway up to the roadway above the boatsheds to Stuart Street. Continue along it as it turns left, rises a hill, crosses Addison Road and drops down the other side. Turn into Craig Avenue which will take you past a charming old weatherboard residence, surrounded by oleander bushes to Little Manly Beach.

Little Pool, Little Manly

This delightful little cove faces south so it's an ideal place when blustery nor'easters blow in summer, or a good position to photograph ferries battling southerly swells in winter. There is a small netted swimming area with the usual taps, swings and toilets. At the eastern end of the beach, walk up steps to the park above and down to the headland where the Manly Gasworks once stood.

In the past small colliers known as 'Sixty Milers' (being the distance from Sydney to Newcastle by sea) brought coal to the site for processing into gas. The Manly Gaslight and Coke Company was formed by 1883 and work started on the gasworks here the following year. After a name change to the Manly Gas Company Ltd it was taken over by the larger North Shore Gas Company. Although it's been many years since gas was produced here (1964) the unmistakable smell lingered on for years.

The amazing 360 degree view from here takes in high home units to the north, towering above the interesting old timber, workers' cottages in the street nearby, past the Manly Hospital to Collins Beach, the Australian Police Staff College, quiet Store Beach (except on weekends when 40 or 50 boats compete for space) and Quarantine Beach, above which is the Old Quarantine Station, first used in 1837, but better known in recent times for housing the refugees from Darwin's Cyclone Tracy in 1974. Nowadays modern drugs have made the station redundant, so this area with its stunning views has

Collins Beach. Leave by the right hand corner

now become part of the Sydney Harbour National Park.

The headland after Quarantine Bay is Cannae Point, named after the Aboriginal name for the Manly area, Canna. Beyond up the Harbour are the eastern suburbs, Bradleys Head, Georges Heights Middle Head, Balmoral, Grotto Point, Dobroyd Head, Manly Point, the twin round units towards Smedleys Point and back to Little Manly Cove.

Having well exercised the neck, walk back around the Collins Beach side pathway and into Stuart Street at the dead end. (If a walk that avoids the rough little tracks and beach is desired, cross Stuart Street to Marshall Street then follow it to the top of the hill where it joins Darley Road. Cross to Vivian Street. Read on till you reach Vivian Street in the text. Then just follow the rest.)

Back at the end of Stuart Street you'll see a pathway that leads between two Norfolk pine trees. Follow this and the steps along the edge of the bay until it peters out at the end of the Cardinal's Palace wall.

We are now in Sydney Harbour National Park, and although the bush track from here to the beach is a bit rough, it isn't a problem. Just walk along until the track drops down sharply to the beach. Climb down and walk across the sand.

In the far corner of the beach is a little waterfall and the two or three steep steps to the left of this will take you past a cement pillar which sometimes (vandals permitting) has a plaque suggesting it was near this place that Governor Arthur Phillip was speared by an Aborigine in 1790.

Phillip had come with George Collins, the Judge's Advocate, to meet up again with his Aboriginal friend Bennelong, who had been on 'walkabout'.

Having found him and shared some wine, Phillip noticed 'a native with a spear in his hand'. The Governor went towards him, dropping his dirk or dagger so as not to alarm him. This seemed to confuse the Aborigine who threw his spear which hit Phillip, the point going clean through his right shoulder, just above the collar bone.

Later the spear was removed and fortunately Governor Phillip recovered fully. The Aborigine, named Wil-ee-ma-rin, was admonished by his peers and all was forgiven. This cove where the drama is believed to have taken place was named after the learned Judge Collins.

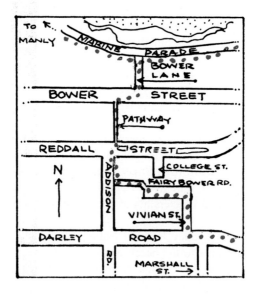

St Patrick's College

Having returned to the present we leave the pillar, turn right onto the track, pass over two little wooden bridges and carry on up to the roadway outside the Australian Police Staff College. (Should the bush track we've just traversed be overgrown, see Trip 2 for information on ticks.) Now just follow the sealed road up the hill through the bush to the top of the ridge where you will join the main road, North Head Scenic Drive. (Watch out for traffic).

Cross to the footpath and continue down past Manly Hospital, St Patrick's College on your right, and on your left the Cardinal's Palace, built as an episcopal residence in the 1850s. Cardinals ranked as princes of the Church, therefore the courtesy title for their dwellings was palace.

Turn right into Vivian Street for a front-on uninterrupted view of the sandstone splendour of the college, before continuing down Fairy Bower Road with its houses of contrasting designs to a laneway beside Moray Manor. At the end turn right, into Addison Road and

Shelly Beach, one of very few northside beaches to face west

continue to its end. Turn right and go on the lower side of Reddall Street and after a row of garages turn down a grassy right of way to a 'No Through Road', Bower Lane.

Pause for lunch at the restaurant (if there is any room) before heading east along the marine pathway. Swim in the pool, or off the beach or rocks in this beautiful area. (Use the outside shower by the toilets above the pool to prevent that salty stickiness on the way home.)

Alternatively walk on up to pretty, secluded Shelly Beach. Then walk up the footpath to the right of the beach past the indoor/outdoor restaurant (unless your appetite, dress and wallet allow otherwise) to the car park above, at the end of which is a path (left) through the low bush to Shelly Point with its sweeping views of Manly, the coast and sea. Should there be a southerly swell, surfboard riders will be zooming down the waves on the northern side of the headland. Owing to Manly's delightful climate with its average temperature of 20° to 27° Celsius in summer and 9° to 18° Celsius in winter this sport is enjoyed all year round.

Where the pathway seems to stop, carry on up over a few rocks to rejoin the path and a short distance on, a lookout seat from where you can 'check out the waves'. Now simply walk back to the car

Waiting for the big one

I wonder what the poor people are doing

Where it all began

. . . A famous part of Australia

park, down to Shelly Beach and around the waterfront, past Fairy
Bower to Manly Surf Pavilion.

Wander along this famous part of Australia where surf bathing
(with the silent 'P') started in 1902. Newspaper editor Mr William
Gocher told one and all through his paper that he was going to defy

The Corso, Manly

the law and surf outside the hours allowed for swimming—8 p.m. to 6 a.m. He did so at noon but was ignored by the boys in blue, and no arrests followed. Thereafter there was no stopping the reckless locals from gambolling in the surf at any hour of the day or night.

The Far West Health Scheme Building on the left hand side of the road not far from the surf pavilion, houses unwell and underprivileged children who come from drier parts of the continent to stay in Manly, where after school they can throw their bodies into the sea — which many of them have never seen.

Cross the road a couple of streets up at a pedestrian crossing near the Visitors' Information Centre and meander down the Corso plaza. The Corso gets its name from a street in Italy with which the 'Father of Manly', Henry Gilbert Smith, was familiar.

Although the village was planned for Balgowlah he saw the potential of the land with surf on one side and quiet harbour waters on the other. In 1842 he purchased over 100 acres (40.5 hectares) at £20 ($40) an acre.

By 1853 Smith was running ferries over from the town to his land, mounting fireworks, sports and band displays, and of course selling land. A year later he built his mansion 'Fairlight House', after which that suburb is named.

Manly Swimming Enclosure, 1933–1974

Having strolled down the Corso we cross to Manly wharf where on the western side we see a small netted area for swimming. Once the whole bay from the wharf across to Oceanworld was enclosed. Slippery slides, water wheels, greasy poles, diving boards and pontoons helped entertain thousands who packed in at weekends and holidays. Admission was free.

The heavy timber enclosure, topped by a broadwalk, was built in 1933 by the Manly and Port Jackson Steamship Company to encourage people to travel on their splendid fleet of steamers. Over many years they did just that.

Then in May 1974, during a storm, a huge swell sent big seas crashing into the structure, damaging it beyond repair, and taking a part of Manly history with it. Twenty years on, a new smaller boardwalk is planned, so perhaps once more, boys will leap from above to bomb the girls in the water below!

Only two more decisions to make now. Should we go by ferry or jetcat? I know it's a tough question to answer, so I'll leave you to it. Good luck.

Circular Quay to the Opera House, through the Royal Botanic Gardens to the Art Gallery

From Utzon's winged dream to Greenway's obvious obelisk

Type of Terrain

All of this walk is on good quality path, and although there are steps, even the odd flight of stairs, children's strollers and, with a good helper and inspired detours, even wheelchairs could traverse this course, but the glasshouse has no provision for the handicapped. The ground is mostly undulating.

Degree of Difficulty 2/10

Summary

This is a walk for everyone. However, some will want to shorten the distance, which is easily done. Just choose what you want to see

Man O' War Steps

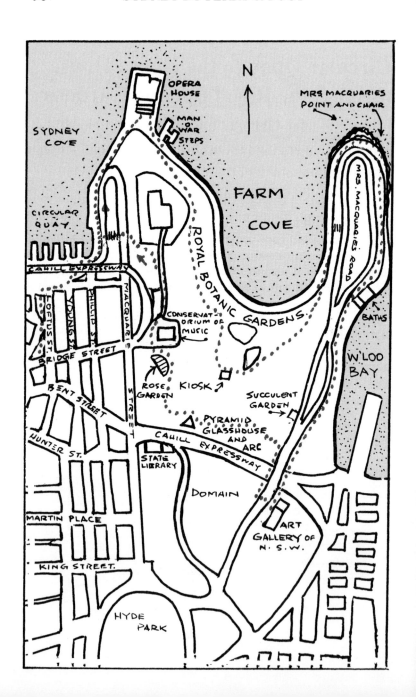

most and head straight for it. You'll still pass interesting scenery whichever way you go.

Beautiful trees and shrubs, harbour views, shipping, art, amazing contrasts in buildings — what more could one ask?

Time
From two and a half hours to almost a day!

Clothes
Hat, sunscreen, reasonable footwear and wind or rain protection as this could turn into a longish day.

Ferry Details
As we start from Circular Quay just catch any ferry that's heading to the city and get off at the Quay, or arrive by train and get off at Circular Quay Station. For Ferry, bus and train timetable information check the current telephone book.

The Walk
Having found yourself at what used to be called 'The Gateway to Sydney', leave the Circular Quay area by taking the roadway towards the Opera House. Just past the second big office building on the right hand side, past the overhead road and railway, notice a flight of stone steps, Moore's Stairs, of 1868, which lead up to Macquarie Street. We'll come down these on our return journey, but for the time being carry on until we arrive at the Sydney Opera House.

While this spectacular structure is now in everyday use, some visitors may be unaware of the controversy encountered during the various construction stages. Danish architect, Joern Utzon's design won the 1956 competition from 222 others. But designing is one thing, building is another, and then there's politics! So it was that many factors combined to complicate an already complex project.

Utzon resigned from the job in 1966, leaving others to complete the interiors. The various opponents had strong opinions about this splendid, controversial and expensive building and several books were written on the subject (most public libraries can provide more information).

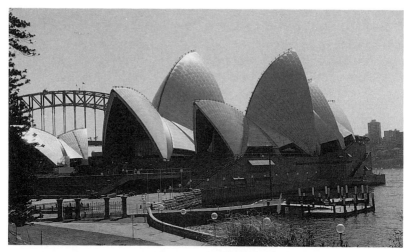

White sails in the sunrise

Moores Stairs of 1868

The Gothic style home of the Governor
of NSW

Luckily for us, however, this world famous arts centre was opened in 1973 and despite all the arguments, today we can see the brilliant sails towering above the harbour, and enjoy the multitude of uses that this unique, Utzon designed Opera House provides.

To make the most of your visit to the building ring 250 7111 to discover what's on the day you plan to go.

Nearby to the east is a wharf known as Man O' War Steps, which has been in use for almost two centuries, since the time of Governor Lachlan Macquarie. It was from these steps that thousands left to join ships in the harbour and fight wars in foreign lands. For many, it was the last touch of Australian soil for good.

Cross the road from Man O' War Steps and go just inside the gates (closed at sunset) and read the map of the Royal Botanic Gardens. Then choose your area of interest and head in that direction. Follow the path along, reading all the names of the various trees and shrubs. Under the ample arms of a Morton Bay fig tree look right for a glimpse between the trees of Government House. It's in the Gothic style, built between 1837 and 1845, and is the residence of the Governor of New South Wales.

The paths diverge here so make your choice. Perhaps we'll go and see the rose garden, then stop at the Kiosk (sit down or take away) for morning tea 10.30 to 12, lunch 12 to 2.30, afternoon tea 2.30 to 4 p.m., which we could eat by the lake while watching the birds.

These gardens are set in 30 hectares (74.10 acres) and are the oldest in Australia, the foundation date being 13 June 1816. The area south of the Macquarie wall has long been known as a spring walk because of the azaleas, wisteria, flowering peaches and annuals that provide a colourful display there in early September. There are also summer, autumn and winter walks for which pamphlets are available at the Visitor Centre. There are free guided walks which are conducted on Wednesdays, Fridays and Sundays, from 10 a.m. (1 p.m. Sundays), except on public holidays, from outside the Visitor Centre near the Woolloomooloo gate—the one nearest the Art Gallery.

Let's move off from the Kiosk area in a northerly direction, which should bring us out at the waterfront path again. Along the way various

The Rose Garden in glorious black and white

Part of the magic of the Royal Botanic Gardens

odours waft up the nostrils. On the day I went these ranged from roses and orange jasmine to Joggers Armpit No.5.

Just through the gates by a flight of stairs is a sandstone memorial to the royal visit of 1954. The wharf used for the landing has since been demolished. Continue on around the bottom path until it divides just around the point. Here you will find the following inscription:

> Be it thus recorded that the road round the inside of the Government Domain called Mrs.Macquarie's Road so named by the Governor on account of her having originally planned it measuring 3 miles [5 kilometres] and 377 yards [345 metres], was finally completed on 13th day of June, 1816.

Just around from the inscription are several seats cut into the face of the rock. The worn one in the centre looks as though it could be old enough for Mrs Macquarie to have rested there all those years ago.

Keep on the centre path for excellent views of Garden Island with its contrasts of charming old colonial buildings and modern naval dockside facilities. Soon you'll see the Andrew 'Boy' Charlton Swimming Pool (named after a famous local world-class swimmer of the

Varied architecture in Woolloomooloo Bay

Coming in for a swim? Mad if you don't!

1920s) looking strangely incongruous among the wharves and business houses of Woolloomooloo.

Carry on across the expressway and enter the Art Gallery of New South Wales. Monday to Sunday 10 a.m. to 5 p.m., closed Good Friday and Christmas Day. Admission is free. It's worth visiting the Gallery at least two or three times a year to enjoy the company of old friends such as the Streetons, Roberts and Conders with their beautiful light quality, or to jump into the more modern paintings, see a new exhibition, study the photographs or the subtle ochres and patterns of the various Aboriginal works. Enquire as to what's showing by ringing 225 1700. Food is available in the gallery restaurant, or in the park café opposite.

If when you eventually leave the Gallery it's a weekday around lunchtime, footballers probably will be breaking kneecaps and elbows in the Domain, or if you're lucky and it's Sunday, eardrums will be at risk instead, as speakers voice opinions on this and that.

Cross back over the expressway bridge and turn back into the Botanic Gardens. Look at the map again just inside the gates and find your way to the excellent succulent garden if there's time. If not head straight across to the Glasshouse complex, which shouldn't be missed. This Glasshouse was the first of its type in the world. It contains orchids, ferns, palms and many other unusual and tropical plants, including some that are endangered or rare in their native habitats.

Modern skyline outside. Ancient exotica inside

Inside it's never cooler than 18°C or warmer than 24°C, and the humidity is always 65° all year round. There are over 500 species of plants (and several fat carp) in this amazing building, which was built in 1972. A second structure was added in 1989.

Head off now in a north-westerly direction towards Macquarie Street, and as we pass still more trees and bushes we notice the effect these beautiful gardens have on visitors, as here and there on the grass are prone figures apparently receiving mouth to mouth resuscitation!

Keep heading roughly north and soon you should be able to make an exit alongside the Conservatorium of Music, with no doubt the odd waft or two from a distant violin, hard at work. When early last century Government House was in need of some stables, Governor Macquarie had Francis Greenway, the ex-convict architect, design the building we now know as the Conservatorium of Music. It was used as stables until 1914, when the courtyard was roofed in to become the Concert Hall.

Cross in front of the 'Con' front doors, pass through the stone and iron gates to the north. Turn left again at the first gate (depot gate), which will bring us out to Macquarie Street. Cross the road, descend the Moore Stairs and cross the road and then wander along the footpath under the overhead road and railway, and cross at the pedestrian crossing in front of the Customs House.

This fine sandstone building was completed in 1885 and is still a

Like a toy castle with musical accompaniment

The Customs House

handsome example of Victorian architecture, despite having been added to and altered. It's worth looking closely at the various excellent carvings and details on the building.

Now walk up Loftus Street to Macquarie Place, where rest some of the last remains of HMS *Sirius* and the 1818 obelisk, designed by Francis Greenway and built by Edward Cureton, a convict stone mason. This is a splendid part of the city, leafy and protected from the winds that can howl up and down the straight main streets. It's surrounded by pleasant warm-looking stone buildings, including the James Barnett designed Lands Department building in Bridge Street which was started in 1877, and surprisingly contains a type of rein-forced concrete.

As it's probably afternoon by now and 'the yard arm crossed' we might just have some refreshment in one of the hotels or taverns around the Quay area. This will leave us with only a short walk back to our homeward bound ferry.

Lunch in the park

Across the Harbour from Circular Quay by Ferry, and by Foot across the Bridge

From the 'Big Coathanger' to old Hangman's Hill

One of the four bearings on which the Bridge rests.

Type of Terrain

This being Sydney, there are hills and steps in this walk but nothing to daunt the reasonably active person. Feel free to drop out after you've crossed the Bridge, although it's almost all down hill from there, the only steep part being the initial climb up from the Harbour onto the Bridge footpath.

Degree of Difficulty 3/10

Summary

After a short trip across the Harbour by a small ferry, we walk around the bottom of the park at Milson's Point, past North Sydney Olympic Pool, up the hill to the Sydney Harbour Bridge stairs, climb these and walk across, all the way to the city. With an interesting detour to Observatory Hill, we visit the home of the National Trust, then walk down stairs and hills, back to the Quay.

Time

Three to four hours.

Sydney Cove

Ferry Departure Details

Hegarty's ferries leave No. 6 Jetty, Circular Quay, about every sixty minutes. Make sure the ferry you catch calls at Jeffrey Street wharf by asking before you board the vessel. (However, the Beulah Street wharf will do equally well. Just walk straight up Beulah Street after leaving the wharf and turn into Kirribilli Avenue.)

Clothes

Comfortable shoes, a hat. Nothing very special is needed for this outing. There are plenty of places to buy snacks and drinks on both sides of the Bridge, but not much shade so don't forget the sunscreen.

The Walk

After the short trip across from the Quay disembark at Jeffrey Street wharf. It was right here that the vehicular punts used to disgorge their load of wagons and trucks which would wind their way up the concrete roadway towards the Northern Suburbs, in the days before the Bridge. Now, beneath our feet, vehicles rush through the harbour tunnel.

We'll turn left and stroll around to the north-eastern pylon, enjoying the best view of the Quay and the city skyline. I wonder how many photographers stood around here to take pictures of the great white passenger liners that passed under the Bridge week after week, right up until fairly recently.

Now go to the western pylon. When you get close enough gaze up at all the Meccano-like pieces of metal which make up (from down here) what seems to be an almost short and fat structure. From other angles further away it looks beautifully slim and fine. Notice also at the bottom of the lower part of the arch the enormous nut that isn't! Made only for appearance, the whole 'nut' and 'washer' can be removed to gain access to the bearing of the hinge pin. There are four of these, and at peak load approximately 20 000 tonnes pushes down on each. Talking figures, the initial three coats of paint used 272 000 litres!

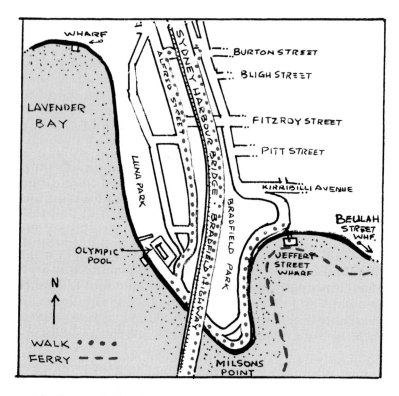

Also here at Milson's Point was the train and tram terminus, as well as the Sydney Ferries Limited depot and workshops. Now we see part of the bow of HMAS *Sydney* and a doric column from the old Sydney GPO.

Amazing how when you're waiting for a train one never comes, and yet there seems to be an ear shattering roar from a crossing train every couple of minutes, especially if you're trapped inside the Olympic Pool at a boring swimming carnival. Pool hours are Monday to Friday 6 a.m. to 9 p.m., Saturday, Sunday and public holidays 7 a.m. to 7 p.m. This is a great pool in summer when the sun bashes down, warming you after a swim, and now in winter too, as the whole pool is covered for warmth and a water temperature of 26°C maintained.

A train every two minutes

Walking too has its ups and downs

Pretty stairs for tired legs

Contrasts in roofing styles

Now walk up Alfred Street to Burton Street, turn right and go through the tunnel and find stairs around the corner. For anyone needing toilets, cross the road from the pool and walk up the centre of the park under the Bridge until the lavatories are reached. They're not always very salubrious. Then walk up Broughton Street until you reach the stairs and the other walkers.

Up we go, and almost immediately the view is that which birds enjoy, and we seem to be unseen and unnoticed by those below. Walk on enjoying the view, the never ending stream of cars, the quite strong shaking of the structure, which makes writing difficult if the page is rested on the railing.

The two closest road lanes used to be tram tracks, which were built strong enough to convert to railway operation as soon as the Manly-Warringah network was built. We're still waiting!

When the centre of the bridge is reached gaze up at the top of the arch and think back to the day when the two halves of the archway were still supported by cables and about to be joined. During the evening a westerly gale sprang up, and with the wind screaming through the girders at 110 kilometres per hour, the Director of Construction, Lawrence Ennis, stood at the top edge of one of the 15 000 tonne arches, watching it and the other half, only millimetres away, swaying in the gusts. He described it as an 'impressive sight'!

As we know now everything held together, the arches were joined on 19 August 1930, and the Bridge officially opened on 19 March 1932. So no more would ferry skippers have to dodge laden barges or have bolts come crashing through the wheelhouse from the workings above.

These days we can get an idea of how high is high by climbing the south-eastern pylon (from 9.30 a.m. to 5.00 p.m., seven day a week). The view is well worth the modest charge.

On we go above Campbell's Cove with its attendant cruise ferries, past the tall brick chimney and the sensible Housing Commission modern units 'Sirius' on Bunkers Hill. As we gaze down on what's known as The Rocks (after the rocky slopes of hereabouts) let's not forget that without the efforts of Jack Mundey and the Builders' Labourers Union most of The Rocks would now be high rise office space! Resident action groups and the Union fought against the plan to build $500 million worth of high-rise buildings in the area in 1973.

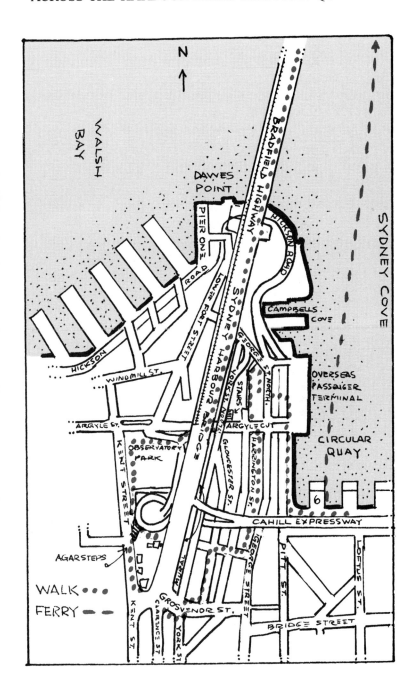

The bird's eye view from the Harbour Bridge

At the end of The Bridge footpath look to the right behind the wire netting and see the barred tunnel (now partly used as a gun firing range) into which trams once rushed on their way to Wynyard. Then after turning left and right go through the archway and down the stairs towards Cumberland Street. Turn right and look behind the fence to enjoy the magnificent mural that turns dull cement into fresh air and sunshine!

Cross over the road and walk back in a northerly direction to the little bridge over Argyle Cut, where you can get down to the pretty Argyle Stairs below. Those with tired legs can leave us here—no don't jump, go down the stairs—past the Glenmore Hotel (unless the throat needs some lubrication of course) down the Argyle Stairs and back to the ferry or via The Rocks if strength and time permit.

We'll retrace our steps back to where we came out of the Harbour Bridge Stairs, and walk through the dingy tunnel to Fort Street and the other side.

Go over to the Observatory Hill Directory and choose your path to Agar Steps. I suggest you go around the Sydney Observatory and along the northern and western boundary of the park. There are excellent views here of the Garrison Church and the neat terraces around Argyle Place. Behind them North Sydney towers up, then around the

From Observatory Hill

Observing the Observatory

skyline Waverton, Lane Cove and various more westerly suburbs are visible. The closest are Balmain and Pyrmont. The tall tower over-looking the Harbour is known as 'The Pill' as it controls all the berths in Sydney Harbour! It is the Maritime Services Board shipping control tower. Wander along under the massive Moreton Bay fig trees and peep in at the Observatory. Built in 1858, it was only ever used for astronomical purposes, except for the ball on top of the tower which used to be dropped at exactly noon as an aid for shipmasters to check their chronometers.

Keep going roughly south past the stairs into the area that contains the S.H. Ervin Museum and Art Gallery. Gallery hours are: 11 a.m. to 5 p.m. Tuesday and Fridays, 2 p.m. to 5 p.m. Saturday and Sunday. Closed Mondays. There is a small charge to enter. There is an excellent bookshop if you go around to the front of the main building, which faces the Bridge approaches; enter by the front door and it's on your right. As this is the home of the National Trust there is a good range of books, mostly referring to buildings, local histories,

Home of the National Trust. Inside is a bookshop, a museum and an art gallery

national parks and the like. It's worth a visit. There's also a coffee shop in this historic building.

It was on this site in 1815 that Governor Macquarie built a two storey brick and stone hospital, traces of which remain in the present building. It was changed in 1848, when it became the 'model' government school, later known as Fort Street. It remained as such until 1974. The extension that houses the Art Gallery was built in 1857.

Go back to the Agar Stairs and walk down, wishing perhaps that more of Sydney's slopes could have looked as pleasant as this building here makes this one.

Go over the road and head south but don't miss looking across to see that stone delight 'Richmond Villa', designed by Mortimer Lewis as his own house in 1882. It was moved stone by stone from its original site in the Domain in 1977-78. It's now the splendid home of the Society of Australian Genealogists. Next door to it is a building known as 'The Ark', thought to have been built around 1820. When Kent Street was cut through 'The Ark' was left sitting high and dry. Hence the name!

Walk to the end of the street past the fire station and IBM Centre and take the pathway to the left which passes under the roads until you come out at York Street. Cross Grosvenor Street and walk down into Gloucester Street, past St Patricks of 1844, Sydney's oldest

Agar Stairs

Why couldn't more of Sydney look like this?

The end of the trip for some. Hangman's Hill

An expensive way to change your view

Catholic church. At the end of this street, turn right into Essex Street and down past the palm trees, where it's thought the first gallows and stocks stood. It seems hard to believe that in this peaceful little part of Sydney people met a sudden and gruesome death, watched no doubt by eager onlookers. (See plaque on north-eastern corner.)

Wander down the street until you reach George Street. Pause here, for on the southern corner of Essex Street stood one of this city's famous old pubs, Jim Buckley's Newcastle Hotel, where writers, artists and poseurs drank and talked back in the 1960s.

Circular Quay is just down the road now, in fact on warm summer afternoons you can smell the salt air from around here. So off you go, or if you feel like a look around The Rocks, now's the time. Carry on down George Street under the roadway (check the map on the wall) and as this is a full-on tourist area, locals may find a fast pace in order. However, then they would miss the interesting little alleys and lanes with their art galleries, craft shops, pubs. museums, etc.

So just find you own way, but try not to miss Cadman's 1816 cottage (almost opposite the Orient Hotel) and the Museum of Contemporary Art, housed in the large sandstone building west of the Quay. There is an admission charge, a café, bookshop etc.

So that's all folks. I'm off to catch my ferry home.

The friendly old Newcastle Hotel run by Jim Buckley. Since demolished

Lavender Bay to Balls Head & McMahons Point

*Where Brett painted in season and Henry wrote
rhyme and reason*

Type of Terrain

From the shores of the Harbour we walk up steep hills and steps to
the top of Union Street, then down again, all on footpaths. At Balls
Head we traverse (mostly) good quality bush tracks before regaining
footpaths and steps which wander up and down hills all the way to
McMahons Point.

The *Koondooloo,* a vehicular ferry in use before the bridge was completed

Degree of Difficulty 3/10

Summary

Interesting suburbia, waterfront and bush with both intimate and sweeping views of Sydney. Lots of nice old houses, unspoiled nature, boats, shipping, something for everyone, except for wheelchairs, strollers and the like, for which the hills and stairs would be too much. Various forms of wildlife visible at times, and the risk from tick bites is low, but read the relevant section in the summary of Trip 2.

Clothes

Good walking shoes should be worn, as should a hat on sunny days and of course sunscreen. As there is nowhere to buy a snack for most of the trip, take something to eat and drink with you, along with any special gear for fishing or whatever. If you want to have a quick swim, you'll have to do so in unprotected waters as all the tidal pools have been closed.

Time

This is a dawdling walk so allow at least three hours. (Ring North Sydney Council, 922 1288, for more information on history and houses.)

Ferry Departure Details

Hegarty's Ferries leave from No. 6 Jetty and run to wharves at Beulah and Jeffrey Streets (Kirribilli), Lavender Bay and McMahon's Point. They all start and finish at Circular Quay. Average frequencies to and from Lavender Bay and McMahon's Point are every 60 minutes.

The Walk

Having been swept around Lavender Bay (named after George Lavender, an early boatman) by ferry, leaving yachts bobbing in our wake, we come ashore at the little Lavender Bay wharf, behind which is a railway line. This line was opened to the northern suburb of Hornsby in 1893, when steam trains would chuff down the North Shore line packed with workers heading for the ferries, which would

Stairs built for the hordes in the days of the steam ferries

From boat building to boat watching

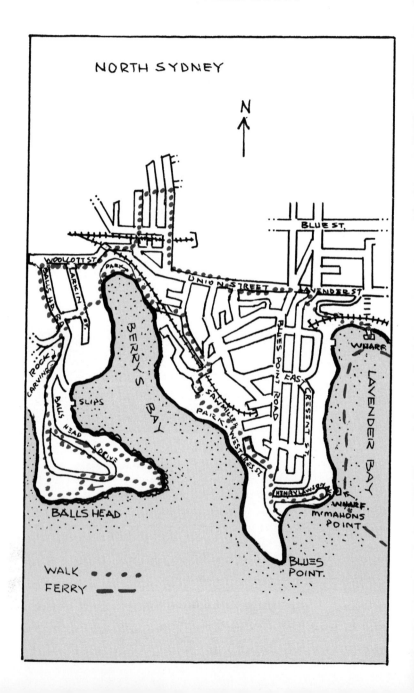

then take them over the water to the city. The line is now only used as a siding for storing trains used during the busy peak hours.

You'll need to walk through the first archway and see the size of the twin paths and stairs to appreciate how many people must have used the big Sydney ferries from the wharf here before the opening of the Bridge. Train, and most tram, passengers used Milson's Point wharf, where Luna Park is now.

More recently, at the top of this path, the late Brett Whiteley made his brush describe the arcs of bridge and bay, amid great daubs of vibrant blue. But we'll retrace our steps and head along the harbour side of the railway line, crossing under at Lavender Crescent.

Then go through serene little Charles Watt Park which looks like something out of the 1960s film *Blow Up*, and climb the stairs at the end of the park.

Serene Charles Watt Park

Cross the road, carry on up more stairs to the top, cross Waiwera Street, then go up and left into Lavender Street and over Blues Point Road at the traffic lights, perhaps stopping at the Old Commodore Tavern for a little refreshment and a look at the nice old North Sydney photos in the saloon bar.

Carry on up Union Street past the building on the left (101) where once many talented people produced films, documentaries and animated series, and where television commercials were churned out like sausages. For on this site and others was once Eric Porter Productions, Sydney's largest film studios. (Architecture enthusiasts

North Sydney Houses

should detour into Chuter Street for a look at a nice group of snug little stone cottages of the 1800s, then return to Union Street.)

Further down on the right hand side is a pleasant large old house, 'Kailoa', which was owned by Sydney Church of England Grammar School (better known as Shore). It was built in the 1880s for Burton Dibbs, the son of Premier Sir George Dibbs. Its once dilapidated state was the result of the owners starting to demolish it for open playing area, and then being stopped by protesting North Sydneyites.

Having passed the shops on the left turn into Bank Street to enjoy the interesting variety of Victorian terraces and cottages there. Towards the end, on the left hand side by the Family Day Care Centre, go down the lane way to Ancrum Street (also worth a look if you're interested in old houses), across the park and playground to Euroka Street. Walk on down the hill (perhaps reminding us of parts of Balmain or Paddington) until at the bottom, on the left by a little park next to the railway line, a plaque, erected by the North Shore Historical Society and Council, informs us thus...

HENRY LAWSON
Lived and wrote of this district in
Nos. 21, 26, 28, 30, 31 Euroka Street
at various times from 1914—1921.
Previously in other North Sydney houses
from 1892.

I wonder what thoughts lurked behind those sad eyes as he wandered these pavements all those years ago.

We'll go under the railway line now, into Woolcott Street and walk along round the sharp corner past the Bowling Club in Waverton Park, up to and across Bay Road to the end of short Horace Street. Navy watchers can see what's alongside at spick and span HMAS *Waterhen,* and which yachts are visiting our town, by looking across towards Berry Island where the visitors moorings are.

Go back to Bay Street now, then walk right on down past the entrance to *Waterhen,* until the road forks off to Ball's Head Reserve. (Named after Henry Ball, Commander of HMS *Supply* of the first fleet.) A short way up the road on the right had side, behind some bushes, is a fenced area with some Aboriginal rock drawings.

Further along the road divides, so take the left fork past the sign reminding us that (with others) Jack Lang, that forthright Premier of NSW, was responsible for the preservation of this area and the work it created during the depression. Continue along by the track on the right hand side of the road as it climbs up into the bush. Can we be just across the water from such a big city? (This is one of the best pieces of Sydney Harbour bushland you could wish to see. Almost no exotic plants and lots of shapely angophoras, wattles, pittosporum, eucalypts, native grass, rock outcrops—delightful! When I wrote the first edition in 1983 I had to bush bash. Now, thanks to North Sydney Council and helpers, it's a beautiful walk.)

Carry on past the cave with a seat inside and wind along this bush track, still much as it would have been hundreds of years ago. Soon we veer left and down to the same roadway we started on. Cross opposite where the stone steps join the road and down to the track below it, on which we go right. Carry on taking the lower way to Ball's Head.

At the edge of this grassy headland can be seen the remaining shells of Aborigines' meals, for it was here that they sat and ate after a day's hunting and fishing—can't say I blame them!

In the centre of the ground behind the grassed area climb the stairs and footpath past a typical Port Jackson fig with its roots intertwined around the sandstone rock, then head left across the clearing to the railing. Shortly after, a track to your right leads to a toilet and taps (across a road) or continue further for a gas barbecue. Take the left or southerly track from here until the stairs. Climb these and keep to the track past the flag pole and on to the rocks at the end of this headland.

This is another of the great Sydney lookouts, where one can see from the great slab of the Royal North Shore Hospital to the north, westwards through Wollstonecraft the Shell Oil Storage Depot, Greenwich, Northwood, Woolwich, Gladesville Bridge, Cockatoo Island, Longnose Point, Birchgrove (Drummoyne behind), Balmain, Mort Bay, more Balmain with silos behind, Goat Island, City and more City, Eastern Suburbs, Harbour Bridge, Blues Point and the Blues Point Tower. Below is some of Sydney Harbour's deepest water, at 38 metres. (The deepest is between Blues and Dawes Point at 49 metres.) From here one can constantly see all sorts of maritime activity, some of which passes almost directly below. This then must be just the place for a mid-week 'Daylight Saving' picnic.

Having dragged yourself away from all this, leave by the stairs which lead down and to the right, past a cave, then head north, keeping the rock face to your right at all times. Ignore all tracks to the left. Soon the path heads back up to the road. Walk on down and retrace our steps to Wood Street on our right.

Typical Sydney foreshore bush

... Then there's Birchgrove, Snails Bay, Balmain

... Goat Island, the City

... The Harbour Bridge and Blues Point

Leura on the slips at Berrys Bay

The two ramps which led traffic onto the vehicular punt at Blues Point

Go down Wood Street, cross Larkin Street and veer left until at the edge of the large rock, then go down the steps which come out near the green toilets which adjoin the footpath. Carry on down the footpath and steps along the front of the Joseph Bugler playing field, at the end of which is a roadway which becomes John Street.

Walk up the hill past the slipway and moored ferries at Stannard Bros' engineering works. All kinds of interesting boats abound in this area of Berrys Bay (named after Alexander Berry, early kindly land-owner and successful businessman).

Having passed under the bridge turn right into Dunbarton Street and follow it all the way along, with the old North Shore railway line on one side and houses on the other, until it comes to a bridge over the railway. Cross and note to our right a very old wooden cottage, built, it is believed, about 1840. Turn left past 1st Lavender Bay Scout Shed and find to the right a zig-zag track which drops down to Sawmiller Reserve at the southern end of which Eaton's Timber Yard stood for 102 years, until closed in 1982.

If refreshments are in order walk up steep French Street to the Blues Point Hotel, or carry on to West Crescent Street, which starts where the park stops. Turn right at its end into Blues Point Road until Henry Lawson Avenue, which will take us around the harbourside to McMahons Point ferry wharf. Lines of trams once filled with pas-sengers here, eager to get home to nearby northern suburbs, in the days before the bridge was built.

We'll just board the ferry now, cruise under the Bridge and return to the Quay.

... and here comes our ferry now

Trip 11

From Circular Quay to
Valentia Street & Hunters Hill

The trip is always interesting, but harder on Sundays

Type of Terrain
Easy walking on mostly good footpaths with one or two steepish hills. A bus can be caught on the last section, if necessary, to help tired legs (except on Sundays).

Degree of Difficulty 3/10

Time
Three to four hours.

Breaking the still evening reflection

Summary

After an interesting ferry trip we disembark at Valentia Street and catch a bus up to the top of Hunters Hill, then walk down and around •what must be some of the most beautiful houses in Australia, surrounded by magnificent trees, bushes and gardens. After a short bush walk we arrive at Harbour parkland complete with a lookout. Then up and over a hill, and down again back to the wharf where we started, and the ferry home.

Mostly though this is a walk about houses, magnificent houses.

Note: Although the ferry now runs on Sundays, the bus doesn't so unless you want to walk up Woolwich Road to Mount Street (see map p.134), better go on a Saturday.

Clothes

Mostly a footpath walk so ordinary footwear, hat and sunscreen. There are not many spots for lunch, so consider the pub or a picnic.

Ferry Departure Details

Ferries don't necessarily leave from the same jetties on weekends as they do on weekdays, or run to the same timetables, so it is always best to check with the Ferry Information Kiosk (opposite No. 4 Jetty) or ring the ferry information number in the current phone book if you are in any doubt as to departure times, jetties or destinations.

Note: The Hunters Hill ferries run approximately every hour on weekdays and Saturdays, every two hour on Sundays.

Bus Information

Route No. 234 meets the ferry at Valentia Street approximately every hour until early evening. Check with bus driver regarding return trip. There is no bus service on Sunday.

Hunters Hill Notes

During the 1840s wealthy French settlers Didier Numa Joubert and his brother Jules bought a large area of land in the Hunters Hill area. (Hunters Hill was probably named after Captain John Hunter of the First Fleet.) It was known as the 'French Village', and dozens of

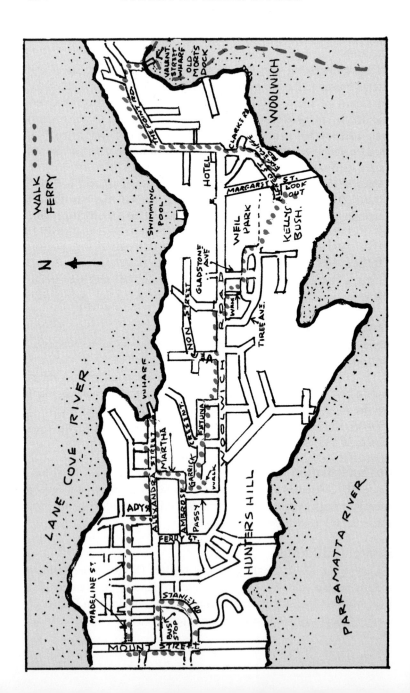

workmen, mostly Italian stonemasons, were brought in to build houses for the Jouberts and others. Local sandstone was used, often quarried on the site. Other Frenchmen were involved with land purchase and house construction: people such as Monsieur Border who imported pre-cut wooden houses, and E.C. Jeanneret who built such splendid houses as 'Lyndcote' and 'Wybalena'.

As the village grew so did the ferry service which had started on a regular basis in 1834. Eventually both Jeanneret and D.Joubert ran ferries to the twelve wharves on the Parramatta and Lane Cove Rivers in the Hunters Hill area. In 1918 the giant Sydney Ferries Limited bought out both the river services and with them the fleet of thirteen 'Lady' class ferries, only one of which, the *Lady Chelmsford,* remains afloat now, in private hands.

By 1946 ferries ran up the Lane Cove River only at peak hours and in 1950 the service was closed, putting an end to the twilight scene of the ferry criss-crossing from wharf to wharf, breaking the still evening reflections, leaving them dancing astern, while the remnants of the bow wave flopped among the rocks. But enough of this nostalgia.

In this outing we'll walk the streets of Hunters Hill and try to get an overall impression of the suburb and its geography. Please remember that the houses we pass are privately owned and on no account must their grounds be entered.

The Walk

Our ferry, having nudged into various wharves, will let us off at Valentia Street. Catch the bus and alight at the Hunters Hill Public School in Alexandra Street. The School House sets the tone for the walk, as even it is constructed of stone with a slate roof. It was built by residents, donated to the Education Department and opened by Sir Henry Parkes in 1870.

Now walk back in the direction from which we came on the bus and turn into Stanley Road, keeping to the left hand side. Soon we'll pass 'Lyndcote', No. 5, built by Jeanneret in 1858, with its three stories (on the Parramatta River side). Almost opposite is 'Eulbertie' of 1857, an early doctor's house. It is now part of the Primary School.

From Stanley Road looking towards the Parramatta River

Take these stairs to Madeline Street

Once a hotel, 'The Gladstone' stands proudly
on the corner of Alexandra and Mount Streets

Continue on now to the end of Stanley Street.

This is probably a good time to point out that there are so many historic and beautiful houses that it would be impossible to name them all, so only a few can be mentioned here. As is the case with North Sydney, Hunters Hill Council and Historical Society have lists of, and walks to, most of the important houses, and those people interested should enquire during business hours at the Town Hall.

Let's turn right into Mount Street now, then cross that road and Church Street, noticing 'The Gladstone' standing proudly on the corner of Alexandra and Mount Streets. Walk down the hill which used to lead to Mount Street wharf and the nearby Avenue Pleasure Grounds, where Hunters Hill High School stands today.

On the right hand side going down the hill are two sets of stairs. Ignore the first old stone flight and take the second that starts by a power pole with a street light attached. These lead to Madeline Street which has many fine houses. Walk right to the end near Brown's Lane and turn right. This turns out to be Ady Street and will bring us out at Alexandra Street again.

Cross the road and look about at the restored buildings. On the corner of Ferry Street as we head east is 'Garibaldi', built by John Cuneo. It housed some of the stonemasons brought to Hunters Hill to build houses. They lived up in the attic rooms.

Wander on down Alexandra Street to the wharf at the bottom of the hill. (For those who can't face the walk down and back up the hill, turn into Martha Street.) Having enjoyed the smells and sights from the wharf, backtrack to Martha Street and join the others, then continue along until we make a dog-leg turn into Passy Avenue. Towards the end of the street is 'Passy', which was built about the middle of last century for the French Consul. It has been considerably altered since. Beside is an unsignposted laneway.

Let's take the laneway, Passy Walk, alongside the old house and follow it behind the houses until it comes out in Garrick Avenue. Turn right and cross Crescent Street to Futuna Street which soon leads to Woolwich Road. Buses run down here about every hour, so if you feel you've seen enough (or your legs have) there's a bus stop just down the road.

Stone ...

... and more stone

Truly a suburb of magnificent buildings

For the rest of us just stroll along Woolwich Road past Tiree Avenue until opposite number 52, where there is a 'no through road' sign. Turn into the laneway along which we walk, turning left at its end into Tiree Avenue. This is a pleasant divided road with a grassed and treed centrepiece, at the end of which is relief for bored children in the small adventure playground to be found in the park.

On we go now by crossing the road towards the Kelly's Bush sign. In the right hand corner find the entrance to the track which leads off into the bush. Follow the pathway as it winds through native bushland, sometimes featuring those popular exotics, the pretty privet, the charming lantana and the luverly blackberry!

We are now at the edge of Kelly's Bush, saved from development by irate locals and sympathetic unionists, who, around 1970, placed the first 'green ban' on the area. This harbourside area is now being developed for parkland.

Leafy paths and bushy gardens, too

Verandahs . . .

. . . laneways

. . . and gateways

. . . intimate

The path soon comes out at Alfred Street steps, where we turn left to see one of the oldest houses in Hunters Hill. It's the first house on the right hand side and was built by John Clarke in 1834. Now go down to the right of the house to the lookout over the water. Return and continue along Alfred Street, Cross Margaret Street past the park with its horses, which is adjacent to the Woolwich Marina. Keep on up Alfred Street which becomes Edgecliffe, enjoying as we go the sweeping views from Drummoyne to Waverton, past Cockatoo Island, Long Nose Point, with the city skyline behind, past a slim, web-like Harbour Bridge to North Sydney.

Now turn right into Clark Road and up a track in the grass under a Port Jackson fig tree behind the army's 35 Water Transport Squadron buildings. Below can be seen a huge slash in the stone. This used

. . . expansive

to be Morts Woolwich Dock. Opened in 1902, it was in use until 1959 when the company went into liquidation. Nearby was Morts Shipbuilding Slipway, where many of the famous Port Jackson and Manly Steamship Company's 'B' ferries were built.

Cross Woolwich Road now and call into the hotel on the corner if the thirst is upon you. Otherwise continue on down Gale Street and turn into the Point Road and follow it along, finding still more amazing houses, until at last we reach Valentia Street. This sounds like a good place to build a wharf, and sure enough down at the end, there it is!

We'll just wait around now for the ferry and our relaxing trip back to town, knowing we won't be unlucky enough to catch the *Kooleen,* a rather nasty little claustrophobic ferry. She was to be the first of many, but proved to be unpopular, so no more were built. She was replaced by one of the catamaran ferries in 1985.

... and original

Balmain from Darling Street Wharf up the Hills to an Old Church, then to Longnose Point via Birchgrove Park

Where we can walk, but ferries always run

Type of Terrain

This is a footpath walk, with some steep hills and a few steps.

Degree of Difficulty 2/10

Summary

After a quick ferry ride under the Bridge we have a suburban walk past lots of nice houses, including the grand and the humble. We walk up main roads, back streets and everything in between. Being one of Sydney's oldest suburbs there is plenty of history about. (Indeed the Balmain Association has produced an excellent walks map of the eastern part of Balmain, which includes the historic buildings, complete with notes, dates etc. For further information call at the Watch House, on Saturdays from 1 to 3 p.m. at 179 Darling Street, or write to the Balmain Association, PO Box 57, Balmain 2041.)

Step back in time at Thames Street Wharf

Clothes

Wear whatever you prefer, taking into account the weather of course. There are shops and some hotels where lunchtime snacks can be purchased.

Time

Allow at least two hours.

Ferry Departure Details

Ferries don't necessarily leave from the same jetties on weekends as they do on weekdays, or run to the same timetables, so it is always best to check with the Ferry Information Kiosk (opposite No. 4 Jetty) or ring the ferry information number in the current telephone book if you are in any doubt as to departure times, jetties or destinations.

Note: The Hunters Hill and Balmain ferries run approximately every hour on weekdays and Saturdays, every two hours on Sundays. Make sure the ferry stops at Longnose Point for your return journey (at which time try to catch the ferry on its outward journey, then you can have a look around the western part of the harbour before returning to Circular Quay).

The Walk

This is a ten-minute ferry ride, under the bridge, around Millers Point to the eastern shore of the Balmain Peninsula. Leave Darling Street Wharf and walk past the first building on your left which was one of Sydney's few waterfront hotels until it was closed in the late 1960s. The next house on the corner, No. 12, was the Waterman's Cottage of 1841. He would row passengers across the water to Millers Point to the east.

When trams ran in Sydney, Darling Street was unique in having a 'dummy' to assist tramcars down the steep hill to the ferry wharf. It worked like this: as the tram pushed a counterweight or 'dummy' car down the slope, a weight was pushed parallel, uphill. It was connected by an underground cable to the 'dummy'. The reverse effect applied when the tram was ascending, as it was pushed up the incline.

Waterman's Cottage of 1841

Former hotel (the Shipwrights' Arms) and waterman's cottage. The saw-toothed
wall indicates that more was to be added to the building at some stage

Turn left into Weston Street with its nice old houses on one side and
Harbour and city skyline on the other. Pass Paul Street which, if you
could remove the cars, would look like you'd stepped back into the
past. On the left is the beginning of Illoura Reserve or Peacock Point
Park (1970). From 1835 till the 1960s, ships were built and repaired
around what is today park area. Now all is quiet and green, where once
there was noise and scrap metal. This nice park is worth exploring,
especially with children. Perhaps another time, and with a picnic lunch.

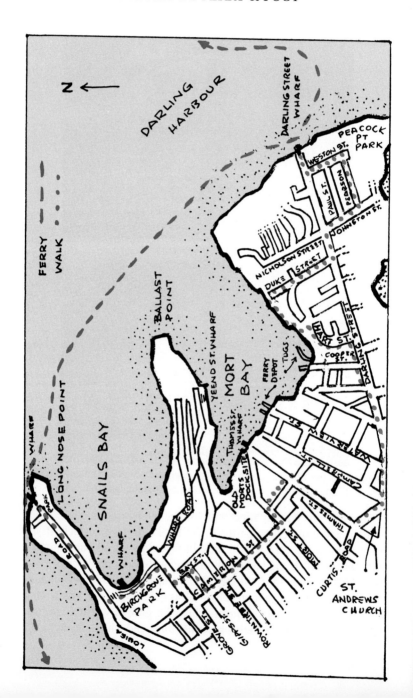

Just past No.7 turn right up the stairs to Pearson Street. At the top of the hill there are two fine old homes, No.11, circa 1844 then, around the corner to the right into Johnston Street, No.12. This magnificent building has been enlarged from its original single storey. Built around 1860, its name has changed from 'Branksea' to 'Onkaparinga'.

Head west now towards Darling Street, where we turn left at the

Paul Street, untouched by time

Magnificent 'Onkaparinga' built about 1860

corner and walk along past the shops and hotel, then cross the road
into Duke Street. This is a short, beautiful and leafy street which
leads into Gilcrest Place. However, continue down Duke Street, turn
left at the end and continue along the waterfront, along the eastern
side of Mort Bay. Ferries have been part of the scene in Mort Bay for
over a hundred years. The Balmain New Ferry Company had its

depot wharves here. They were taken over by Sydney Ferries Limited in 1918. The latter company moored its various vessels here after the Sydney Harbour Bridge construction authority took over their depot at Milsons Point. The yard is now run by the State Transit Authority.

Leave the waterfront by crossing the park opposite the first ship's propeller, and then just follow Hart Street back to Darling Street. Hereabouts the air is heavy with the pong from the Colgate factory at

There have been ferries at the bottom of some Balmain gardens
for over one hundred years

the bottom of Colgate Street. Now walk quickly up Darling, past an
old (1858) sweetshop (No.155), now a house, on the corner of St
Andrews Street. A bit further up is No.177 of 1843, which is believed to have been built for a barrel of rum!

Now we reach Balmain Watch House of 1854. This pleasant old
lock-up is only open on Saturdays between 1 and 3 p.m. However,

The Balmain Watch House of 1854

Built for a barrel of rum!

try to time it so you can manage to look over this historic building. Afterwards you may wish to have that picnic at Peacock Point Park, or in Gladstone Park opposite the church further on.

Carry on up Darling Street, noticing the interesting shops and houses on both sides of the street, including the corner buildings and

St Andrews Congregational Church on a non-market day

a stone and timber cottage in Queens Place. Soon we reach Curtis Road. The choice here is to sample a glass of the many brands of Aussie beers on tap at the London Hotel, or if it's Saturday, wander through St Andrews Congregational Church (1853). It's here that the Balmain Markets are held each Saturday, 9 a.m. to 4 p.m. They have general stalls of clothes, books, records etc., as well as an amazing variety of interesting food to eat, available inside the building itself.

On we go down Curtis Road until Thames Street, into which we turn right, passing the Christian Brothers School and the Salvation Army Home. At Trouton Street look down by the water to Thames Street wharf, which is the last of the type that once were common in many parts of the Harbour.

Head on down Trouton Street to Mort Street, pausing to look at the old hotel, the Forth and Clyde. This attractive building has been well restored and is now used as offices.

Opposite is what used to be the Tasmanian Shipping Terminal. From here the *Empress of Australia* (renamed *Royal Pacific* and sunk in a collision 1992.) and various container ships set out for the Apple Isle. This area is where the old Morts Dock stood, now used for family houses with a pleasant waterfront park adjacent.

The old Forth and Clyde Hotel, now in use as offices

Thomas Sutcliffe Mort made a small fortune from his business activities, and in 1854 decided to build Sydney's first big dry dock. Later workshops and slipways were erected, and after a few years over 700 men were employed here. After Mort died in 1878 his company continued to expand. However, after the Second World War business declined and the works were closed in 1959.

We'll go up Mort Street only as far as Cameron Street. Turn right here, and continue along past the Dry Dock Hotel. In the 1970s, residents fought in these streets with heavy trucks, which rumbled down at all hours, loaded with containers bound for the ships at the Terminal.

Today the Tasmanian passenger ship leaves from Melbourne, and container ships from Botany Bay. These streets are much quieter now.

Birchgrove Park on one side and a row of terrace houses on the other

At the top of the hill cross Rowntree Street and turn right into Gipps Street. Wander down to Bay Street and turn left to Grove. Turn right now and with Birchgrove Park on one side and several rows of terraces on the other, continue on. Just past the bus shelter go left and follow the path along the waterfront, past pretty Snails Bay, its boatsheds and a tiny beach. Climb the stairs to Louisa Road. Turn right and follow this narrow road along until the park is reached. This area used to be part of Morrison and Sinclair, Shipbuilders, and

Quiet corner on Snails Bay

The slipway that launched some fine old Sydney ferries

is worth having a look at. For over 80 years lots of famous boats slid down the 'ways from here, including many of Sydney's steam ferries.

Walk down the steps now, and when the ferry comes hop on smartly, as this is a difficult wharf for the ferry skipper to get alongside when the tide is running hard.

So that's it, all you have to do now, is to find your way home. Good luck!

At last, our ferry home.

Oh, and don't forget that if the ferry is on its outward journey, jump on anyway and enjoy the rest of your trip as the ferry makes a westerly loop before returning to the Quay.

Watsons Bay to Vaucluse via South Head and The Gap

Past grey cliffs, blue waters and brown bottoms

Type of Terrain

Mostly on good footpaths, except for the South Head section which has variable surfaces, steps and stairs and is quite steep in places.

Degree of Difficulty 3/10

Summary

We start at the ferry wharf, continue along the foreshore past Camp Cove and Lady Bay, then on bush tracks and stairs over the headland

The entrance to Sydney Harbour

to the Hornby Lighthouse on South Head. Then return by the same way. (This is National Parks territory so no dogs allowed.) After looking at The Gap we can finish the walk, or continue on footpaths to the majestic Macquarie Light. From there we can go downhill to Vaucluse House, Parsley Bay, then along the waterfront to catch the ferry back to the Quay via Taronga Zoo Wharf (weekends only)

So this is about stunning harbour and ocean views (often windy), cliffs, stunted bushland, wealthy suburbia, harbourside parkland, tidal swimming pools, and several places to eat and drink. Sound good? Then let's go!

Clothes

Please yourself on this one, but don't forget sunscreen, perhaps a towel and swimming costume or a windcheater.

Time

First part about 3 hours—whole walk, all day.

Ferry Departure Details

This used to be a weekend only service, but ferries now run on a limited weekday timetable as well. On weekdays the service is less frequent with no stops at the Zoo. Check the timetable by asking at the ferry Information Kiosk at the Quay or by ringing the Ferry Info Line number in the current telephone book. There is also a bus service from Circular Quay to Watsons Bay.

Doyles restaurant runs a water taxi service to Watsons Bay on weekdays—check at the wharf or at the Commissioners Steps on the western side of Circular Quay.

Bus Information

Route 324, 325 from Circular Quay to Watsons Bay via Rose Bay and return, at least every 30 minutes, including weekends.

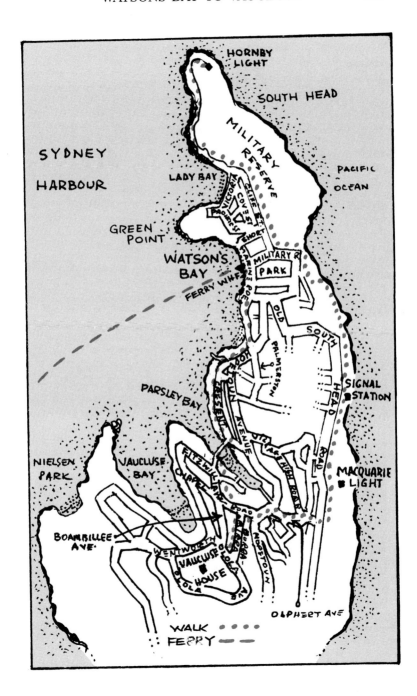

Doyles and dinghies

Wharves and water

Lovely Lady Bay

Striped lighthouse

The Walk

So here we are at Watsons Bay, named after Robert Watson, Quartermaster in HMS *Sirius* of the First Fleet. In 1811 he became Harbour Master/Pilot and the first keeper of the Macquarie Lighthouse when it first blinked into life in 1817. (It was to Watsons Bay that the ferry *Greycliffe* was heading when she was run down and sunk in 1927. (See Trip 3 for details.) At the end of the wharf is Doyles Fisherman's Wharf Restaurant where we could buy some seafood now or wait until we come past again in the next hour or two. By then a cold drink will probably be in order as well. So to start we'll wander past the hotel, Doyles other restaurant, and along the waterfront walkway. Pass by rows of upturned dinghies and the fleet of moored motor launches. Over these can be seen an unusual angle of the city skyline, and the Harbour Bridge arch peeping over the trees on Bradleys Head.

Turn right at the walkway end and up into Cove Street, then left into Pacific Street which will take us to Green (or Laings) Point and pretty Camp Cove. This is a great place early or late in the summer as it is one of the few Sydney beaches that face west and so gets the sun until relatively late in the day. (I wonder if Captain Phillip and the lads plunged in for a bit of a dip on that warm January day in 1788 when they set up camp here for a couple of days while they explored the coves and bays of the harbour.)

While we're here at Green Point take a stroll out past the public lavatories to the end of the point, and look down near the rocks where odd pieces of concrete indicate where wartime buildings stood, that were associated with RAN's harbour defence submarine boom net. This stretched from here to Georges Head opposite via the Sow and Pigs reef. (Now marked by tower marker buoys, since the old tripod warning mast was knocked over during a storm in 1986). Behind them is Obelisk Bay and Beach, with one of the two white obelisks that were used as guides or leads for vessels entering the harbour.

Having returned to the area near the monument commemorating the landing by Governor Phillip, we can either walk down the steps, along the beach to its end, then up the stairs under a Port Jackson fig tree, or we can end up at the same place by retracing our steps to Victoria Street. Then turn left into Cliff Street. (Notice the well kept Victorian cottage at the north-western end of Pacific Street where the first marine biological station in the southern hemisphere was established by the handily named Russian, Nicolai Nocolaevich de Miklouho-Maclay in 1881.)

Now follow the path up to the old cannon and continue around the cliff top by following the hand rail until the track brings us to Sydney's nude beach. (We pass close to the beach, so anyone offended by the sight of those clad only in their 'birthday suits' be warned!) Let's continue up, and then along from the beach area past wind-pruned bush, behind a couple of old stone cottages until we arrive at the Hornby Lighthouse. From here there must be one of the best views of Sydney Harbour and the ocean, starting at the Main Harbour, then to Middle Harbour, North Harbour, Manly Cove, The Heads and Pacific Ocean, which no doubt is one of the reasons why the Hornby Light was erected here in 1858. After a good look about we'll retrace our footsteps back to Camp Cove past the little kiosk, along Cliff Street until we come to the large park at its end. Perhaps it's time now for a refreshing little drop of something at the Watsons Bay Hotel, followed by some freshly cooked sea creatures from Fisherman's Wharf.

Thus replenished we'll head up to the bus terminus (past the toilets), cross the road and up the steps to the path. This is The Gap, and a short distance along is the anchor from the *Dunbar*. She was a sailing ship of 1321 tons, and just before midnight on 20 August 1857 she was caught in an easterly gale. Heading for the Heads in pitch darkness (for they had passed the Macquarie Light high on South Head) they miscalculated their entry, there being no other guiding light. The ship was driven onto the rocks just below The Gap and the *Dunbar* quickly broke up. Only one survivor, James Johnson, made it ashore out of 122 aboard. (Nine years later at Newcastle Harbour he helped rescue the only survivor from another shipwreck). They weren't the only ones to lose their lives near here, as this is the most 'popular' place in Sydney to come and end it all. Over the years many would-be suicides have been talked out of taking the big step

The Gap

The Eastern Suburbs Flasher

by police, tram and bus crews etc, but many dozens more have succeeded in taking the plunge.

In our case too, this is a good time to decide to carry on or turn back.

Those who want to see more follow the footpath past the last of the bush on our right (where trams wound their way down to the bay, before their demise in 1960) and then on up Old South Head Road to the Signal Station. Ever since 1790 someone has been present here contacting incoming shipping, keeping watch, and since the 1840s doing so from this very building: (Now manned by the Australian Volunteer Coast Guard Assoc.)

On we go a few hundred metres to the Macquarie Light. This really is a beautiful, clean, classic lighthouse. Australia's first, it was built in 1818 (replacing a fire which was lit nightly). Designed by the convict architect Francis Greenway, who was pardoned on its completion. By 1880 the stonework had deteriorated so badly in this exposed position that a new lighthouse was built to the same design alongside the original.

Let's press on almost to the end of the park and cross at the pedestrian crossing near the grandstand and carry on down Village High Road, and then follow Olphert Avenue to its western corner. There, in a group of three garages, find a pathway with a street visible at its end. This is Hopetoun Avenue which we cross. Now those who want to visit Vaucluse House, enter Fitzwilliam Road almost opposite. Then a short distance down, go left into Burrabirra Avenue and at its end cross Olola Avenue and walk down the hill until you find the entrance to Vaucluse House

This fine old building was rebuilt incorporating an older cottage in 1827, by William Charles Wentworth. It is in beautiful condition and contains all sorts of interesting colonial furniture and artefacts. It opens Tuesday to Sunday 10 a.m. to 4.30 p.m., closed Monday (except public holidays). Leave by the Wentworth Road exit if you want to catch the bus from here (Route 325), otherwise leave by crossing Olola Avenue into Boambillee Avenue then continue in a northerly direction, cross over Chapel Road into Fitzwilliam, where on the right hand side past Parsley Road, you'll find steps which lead down to a path. At its end, cross the suspension bridge over the enclosed pool at Parsley Bay Reserve.

For those who didn't come to Vaucluse House, after crossing Hopetoun Avenue turn right, then wander around the curve and down the pathway marked 'To Parsley Bay'. This passes back yards and bush until we reach this beautiful secluded little bay. Swim in the netted pool or just rest before heading back.

O.K., let's meet the Vaucluse House mob on the northern side of the bridge, and head up the steps and along The Crescent until we reach Hopetoun Avenue again. Turn left down Palmerston Street which

Vaucluse House

Anyone for tea?

leads us to a waterfront walk, Marine Parade, pilot launches and a last chance for a swim in the public pool, or maybe a little reviver in the Tea Gardens opposite. Pass the stone obelisk celebrating the completion of the road from here to Sydney in 1811, which was finished in ten weeks! Just a little further along is another antique building. Built before 1840, Dunbar House has been a private house, hotel, council chambers and a restaurant.

That's it then. Finished. We'll just dawdle around to the wharf, board the ferry, and sit down at last for the cool, refreshing trip back to the Quay. On weekdays, Northsiders may prefer to get off at Taronga Wharf instead. The rest is up to you.

Trip 14

Watsons Bay to Rose Bay via Nielsen Park

Where boats used to fly—seagulls now cry

Type of Terrain

Almost all hilly footpaths but with stairs, rough stone steps and bush tracks.

Degree of Difficulty 3/10

Summary

From the wharf we soon leave the harbour, but return at intervals throughout the walk. Swimming and picnic areas abound, from Watsons Bay itself, through Parsley Bay, Vaucluse Bay, Neilson Park, along the Hermitage Walk and Rose Bay. Takeaway food and drinks at Watsons Bay and Nielson Park. Detour to see charming Vaucluse House.

Time

About three hours.

Fasten your seat belts

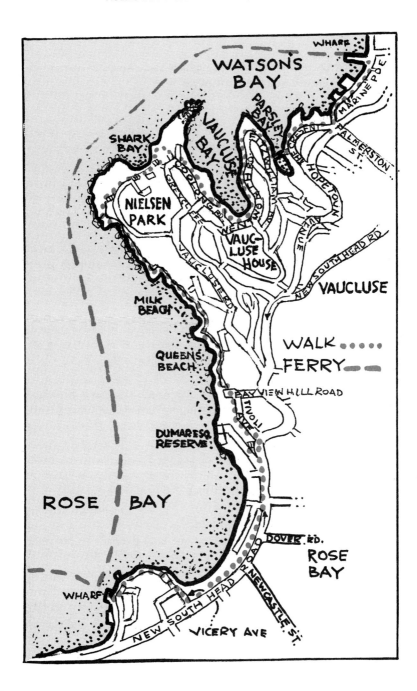

Clothes

Hat, sunscreen, robust shoes and perhaps some kind of wind protection, as we head south for most of the time.

Ferry Departure Details

The Watsons Bay weekend and holiday service usually leaves from No.4 Jetty, with calls at Taronga Zoo and Rose Bay en route, leaving at about one and a half hourly intervals, from about 9am until 5pm. On weekdays the service is less frequent with no stops at the Zoo. Check the timetable by asking at the ferry Information Kiosk at the Quay or by ringing the Ferry Info Line number in the current telephone book.

Doyles restaurant runs a water taxi service to Watsons Bay on weekdays—check at the wharf or at the Commissioners Steps on the western side of Circular Quay.

The Walk

Note: The walk could be reversed by starting at Rose Bay, but as there is only a limited weekday ferry service to Watsons Bay, I feel it's best to Start there, to make sure of catching a ferry home late in the day.

Having decided not to walk to South Head, lets leave the wharf, and the temptations of food and drink, by turning right into Marine Parade under the huge, leafy old fig trees, past stately Dunbar House, the obelisk and tearooms (details of which can be found at the end of Trip 13). Continue to almost the end of the Parade, then turn up the pathway past the Pilot Station, which becomes Palmerston Street. At the top go right into Hopeton Avenue. All is quiet about these mansions except for the sounds of hired help at work outside, and the faint jangle of jewellery from within.

Cross into The Crescent and continue until the park on the right, take the first pathway for views of the harbour and Clifton Gardens to the southwest and Parsley Bay below. Stay on the top path and then cross the delightfully quaint suspension bridge and at the top of the pathway, turn right into Fitzwilliam Road and carry on into Wentworth Road (noticing the bus stop grotto, flagpole and cannon on the corner) before following the road around and down into the grassed area of Vaucluse Bay. Vaucluse House visitors (for details see Trip 13) may cross the road here, but we'll push on by taking the first road (Coolong Road) to the right.

Soon we come to a green hill ahead which turns out to be Nielson Park. Take the first park road on our right, around past the glittering harbour, then down steps past the womens toilets and showers (the mens are below) to the beachfront. What a beautiful old park this really is. With its netted pool, sandy beach (called Shark Beach—no wonder the pool is netted!), charming cottage-like kiosk and tea rooms, huge changing sheds, ancient trees and in the cooler months, particularly nice as the sun shines all afternoon.

Now climb the steepish stairs at the southern end (past more toilets) and carry on until you reach the Hermitage Foreshore Walk. Check the map at the top of the steps, then down you go. This is a splendid, intimate meander, up hill and down dale, through leady glades, past little, still beaches (like Milk and Queens) lots of lookouts with amazing views up the harbour, hence all the posh houses (or should that be grand residences?) about the place.

Foreshore

Unfortunately, the track stops at Hill View Lane. What a pity as it seems not too difficult a job to continue along the waterfront with a wooden walkway (the way Manly Council has done between The Spit and Clontarf).

We, though, have to cross from Hill View Lane and Road into Tivoli Avenue, at the end of which one can wander on down South Head Road, around the curves and after passing through Rose Bay shopping centre, at the southern end of which once stood one of Sydney's finest picture theatres, the Wintergarden, we turn right into Vickery Avenue. (However, a way can be found around the waterfront at low tide, from Dumaresq Reserve. Take the first set of public stairs after Tivoli Avenue, then turn right into Dumaresq Road. From the park follow the edge of the sand all the way to Rose Bay. It's soggy in places so it is a barefoot job.

O.K. So now we'll all end up in Vickery Avenue and join the path in front of the sailing club where, nearby, until the 1970s the slow but beautiful flying boats left at all hours to catch the tide at Lord Howe Island. Today smaller seaplanes head north from hereabouts. We have to catch a ferry instead, and thankfully the wharf is just around the corner, so now it's time to rest the legs and sit and dream of flying through the clouds to some exotic paradise—hang on, that sounds like this very harbour to me!

The Hermitage

Circular Quay to Meadowbank, via Drummoyne, Gladesville and Abbotsford

Today to Meadowbank, tomorrow the Olympics

Note: This is mostly an excuse to explore the Parramatta River by ferry. However, as several wharves have pleasant picnic areas nearby, we'll look at them as we go.

Type of Terrain
Naturally this varies at each location, but parents with children in strollers or people in wheelchairs should have no trouble, although

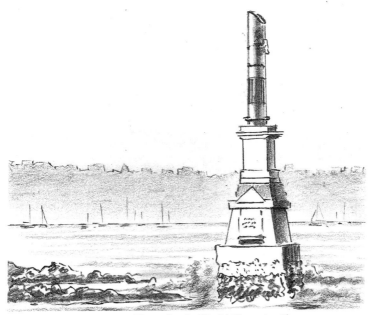

A monument to Henry Searle, World Champion Rower

some of the access tracks to the picnic areas are steep, narrow and rough. There's a bike/walking track which is reasonably flat which winds along the banks of the river near parkland and playing fields. Also, at Gladesville there is a steep flight of stairs to climb directly after leaving the wharf.

Degree of Difficulty 2/10

Summary
The ferry stops at McMahons Point or Darling Harbour on weekends, Wolseley Street, Drummoyne, Gladesville, Abbotsford and Meadowbank. It then returns, calling at the same wharves. We'll have a look and see where's best for a picnic by the river.
 Note: Beware of the famished mosquitoes at Meadowbank Park. Take some insect repellent during the summer months.

Clothes
Hat, sunscreen, robust shoes and perhaps some wind protection. No food is available at Meadowbank, so why not take a picnic to one of the parks.

Time
As all the picnic areas are within about ten minutes walk (except Henry Lawson's which is about 20 minutes), the time taken will depend on how long you spend over lunch.

Ferry Departure Details
There is a reduced service on weekends, so check with the ferry information kiosk at Circular Quay before departure or ring the Ferry Info Line listed in the current telephone book.

Bus Details
Route 438 Abbotsford to Circular Quay at least every 30 minutes.

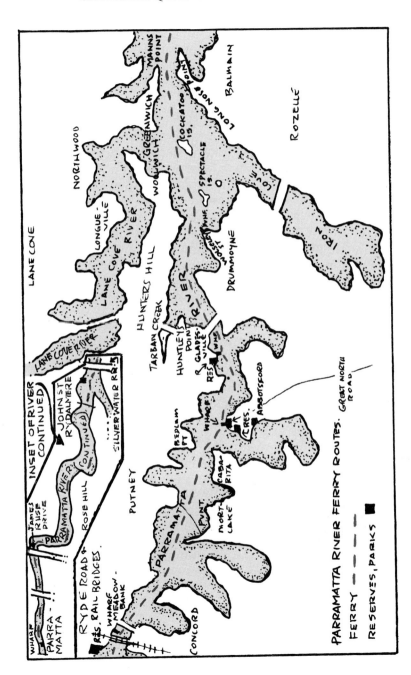

PARRAMATTA RIVER FERRY ROUTES.

FERRY – – –

RESERVES, PARKS ■

Train Details

Regular suburban electric trains run from Meadowbank station.

The Walks

On weekdays, the first stop for the ferry after leaving Sydney is McMahons Point (Darling Harbour on weekends), but as it doesn't set down passengers when westbound, and as there is already a walk in this area (Trip 10) we'll stay on board.

We cross into the Parramatta River when we pass between Longnose Point and Manns Point. Then we make a turn to port (left), pass behind Cockatoo and Spectacle Islands before stopping at suburban Wolseley Street. Lots of houses hereabouts so we'll press on under the arch of Gladesville Bridge and maybe get off at Gladesville Wharf. From here we could climb the stairs, and by keeping to the left at the top wander along into Gladesville Reserve. There's nothing special about this bushy little park. There's the odd shelter, it's a bit overgrown and is really only an adjunct to the nearby playing fields.

So on second thoughts let's stay on the ferry, and soon after passing the stone abutment of the old Gladesville Bridge we swing around the shore at Henley. On our right is a broken column which

Gladesville Wharf

is Searle's Monument. It is mounted on dangerous rocks known as 'The Brothers', and was also used to mark the end of the rowing course, which started at the Ryde Bridge.

Until the mid to late 1800s professional rowing was the most popular sport in Sydney, attracting huge crowds to the river. One of their heroes was Henry Searle. he came to Sydney in 1888 and the same year became world champion at 22 years of age. In England the following year he successfully defended his title. Tragically when homeward bound he contracted enteric fever and died shortly after his arrival in Australia. It is believed that a quarter of a million Sydneysiders turned out to pay tribute to the great sculler as his coffin passed through the streets on its way back to his home on the Clarence river. The cost of his memorial was met by public subscription. In 1994 it was mysteriously knocked over and badly damaged.

The next ferry stop is on the southern side of the river at Abbotsford Wharf. In days past this was the most direct way to the Hunter and Hawkesbury districts. Here at the end of the Great North Road a punt took travellers across to Bedlam Point, where they continued on the journey. (It was named Bedlam Point because a 'lunatic asylum' stood there).

Let's get off the ferry here for there's a choice of three parks nearby, or we could hire a launch from the boatshed by the wharf and explore the river more thoroughly, or just sit about and fish. Also right by the wharf is Werrell Reserve which has the usual park furniture of tables and seats, childrens playground etc. plus one coin-operated electric barbecue. It is a well kept area with nice shady trees and trimmed grass. Access is by steps or by roadway and footpath.

If you would like to get even closer to the water or you'd like more space, walk up the road from the wharf a short distance and take the first on your right, which is The Terrace. This will take you down to Battersea Park. Here we have two coin-operated electric 'barbies', tables, toilets, taps and a modern childrens playground.

There's yet another smaller park you can reach by walking along Great North Road as far as the shops. Turn right into Abbotsford

Parade, which leads to Henry Lawson Park (named of course for one of the best known Australian poet/writers who lived nearby for the latter part of his life until his death in 1922). Here, there are also a couple of electric 'barbies', tables and a concrete cricket pitch. Not a great place to be in winter though, as the southerly wind blows straight in. Still, a benefit of the parks in this area is that should you miss the last ferry there's always the 438 bus back to Circular Quay. We'll retrace our steps back to the wharf.

The ferry continues up river from here, soon passing Cabarita Point. Should the ferry stop here in future there's an olympic type pool, an historic pavilion, parks, gardens etc. and a boating marina with boat hire and refreshments. A little further on, on the same side of the water is Mortlake where once the Australian Gaslight Company's gas holders stood out against the sky. In the days before natural gas three colliers supplied these works with almost half a million tons of coal annually.

Some warning blasts from our ferry indicate that we're about to cross the path of the Mortlake to Putney vehicular punt. Shortly after we pass a headland on our left with an ornate brick building right on the waterfront. This is the gatehouse of the Thomas Walker Convalescent Hospital. On the right hand side is the Royal Australian Navy's Small Ship Repair Facility, originally owned by the Halvorsen boatbuilding family. Then it's under the Ryde Road bridge and up to the Meadowbank wharf.

If it's lunchtime or if you want to walk about for a couple of hours, go left away from the wharf, under the railway bridge and follow the path. Up on the right in Meadowbank Park are tables, coin-operated barbecues and a childrens playground.

After lunch there's a pleasant stroll on a path which wanders along the river's edge, but don't forget the insect repellent. These mozzies don't mind feeding even as you walk (in summer)!

Circular Quay to Historic Parramatta

To go west, it's best, on a rivercat

Type of Terrain

Mostly flat ground means that apart from a few steps here and there, this is a walk for anybody. However, for those keen (or able) there is (at the time of writing) an explorer bus which meets the ferry, takes you to the important houses, and picks you up afterwards.

Degree of Difficulty 2/10

Clothes: See trip 15.

Summary

What a unique experience for Sydneysiders and visitors alike to be able to zoom up the harbour then wind around the narrow river in the fast rivercat, and this trip gives you two goes at it as well, plus

Bronzewing, an early Parramatta River ferry.

something interesting to do when you get there.

So this is about an exciting ferry trip and the opportunity to visit some of Australia's oldest buildings—and for a few dollars, go inside and see what living was like almost 200 years ago.

Time
If you want to walk to a house or two, you'd better allow a day for the round trip.

Ferry Departure Details
The weekend and weekday services offer about the same number of trips but sometimes the weekend boats fill quickly so get to the Quay in good time. If you want to join the ferry at an upriver wharf, check with the ferry information number listed in the current telephone book, as stops vary during the day.

Bus and Train Details
There are regular train and bus services to and from Parramatta. Check at the visitors centre (630 3703) for up-to-date information.

The Walks
For descriptions of the river journey as far as Meadowbank, read Trip 15. From there the river runs through flat industrial and residential country until the waterway narrows dramatically, and we slowly wind our way through the mangroves and under bridges until we reach Parramatta.

Parramatta has an abundance of old, well cared for buildings of various types and is an attractive city just to wander about in. So unless you want to sit in the park and wait for the next ferry, the first place to head for is the Visitors Centre (or ring before you leave home) as here you can plan the walk that suits you. There are over 20 buildings of interest to see, of which four or five are open most days of the week. The most popular houses are as follows.

• Old Government House. The oldest public building in Australia. Open Tuesday to Thursday 10 a.m. to 4 p.m. Sundays and public holidays 11 a.m. to 4 p.m. Cost $5; child/concession $3. Parramatta Park, cnr Pitt and Macquarie Streets.

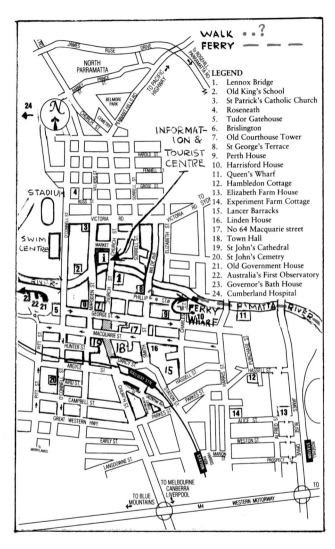

Parramatta showing the four most popular houses that are open to the public, numbers 12,13, 14, 21. (original map courtesy Parramatta Visitors Centre, open weekdays and Saturdays 9 a.m. to 1 p.m., Sundays 10.30 a.m. to 3 p.m. Telephone 630 3703

• Elizabeth Farm. A political, social and agricultural centre of early NSW. Gardens, lunch and teas. Tuesday to Sunday and public holidays 10 a.m. to 4.30 p.m. Costs as above. 70 Alice Street, Granville.

• Experiment Farm Cottage. The colony's first land grant. Tuesday to Thursday 10 a.m. to 4 p.m. Sundays and public holidays 11 a.m. to 4 p.m. Cost $4; child/concession $3. 9 Ruse Street.

• Hambledon Cottage. Built for the governess to the Macarthurs' three daughters. Wednesday, Thursday, Saturday, Sunday and public holidays 11 a.m. to 4 p.m. Cost $2.50; concession $2; child $1.50. Hassall Street.

Right, lets go! Head for the grand old houses straight away if you think you can find them. (There's a small map included so slip on the specs and see how you go.) Otherwise, we'll leave the park by heading west and into Phillip Street until the second on the right which is Church Street. Go right here and then on the left just over the river, opposite the distinctive Gazebo Hotel is the Visitors Centre. Here you will find all the necessary information to spend a day or an hour or two in this old by pretty city of Parramatta. Also, should you want to be advised of an alternative way home (though I can't imagine why!) this is the place.

I know which way I'll be going back. Perhaps I'll see you out the front of the ferry—Bye.

Through the mangroves to Parramatta

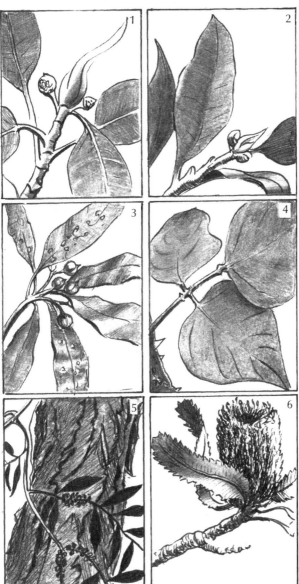

1. **Moreton Bay Fig**, Actual leaf size 16-20cm

2. **Port Jackson Fig,** actual leaf size approx 8-10cm

3. **Pittosporum** 10-12cm leaf size, yellow fruit, pale perfumed flowers in early spring

4. **Coral Tree**, long thin red flowers in winter, leaf size 12-14cm

5. **Paper Bark** (Melaleuca), leaf size 8-10cm.

6. **Banksia**, leaf size 14-16cm

Leaves of the **Angophora** (top) symetrically arranged and the staggared leaves of the **Eucalyptus**.

Casuarina or She-oak with 'leaves' like pine needles.

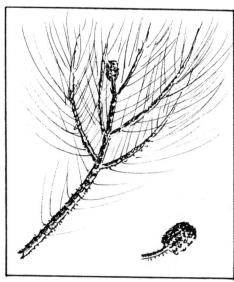

Index

★

BIBLIOGRAPHY

A Pictorial History of Mosman, Rob Sturrock, Rotary

The History and Description of Sydney Harbour, P.R.Stephensen, Rigby

Across the Harbour, John Gunter, Rigby

The Companion Guide to Sydney, Ruth Park, Collins

The Romance of an Old Whaling Station, E.A.Archer, Mosman Historical Society

The Manly Warringah Story, C.E.McDonald and Capt. C.W.T.Henderson, Hamlyn

Trolley Wire, S.P.E.R.

An Abbreviated History of Hunters Hill 1835-1977, Hunters Hill Historical Society

Main Roads Magazine, D.M.R.

Balmain Walks I, The Balmain Association

The Royal Botanic Gardens, Sydney, A pamphlet from the Gardens Visitor Centre